For Pastor Anne,

From Esther with love

November 2017

Each Life is
A BCDE!

## Each Life is A BCDE!

**초판 1쇄 발행** (First Printing) 2017년 11월 13일 (November 13, 2017)

**지은이** (Author)_ 손은정 (Eun-Jeong Sohn)
**펴낸이** (Publisher)_ 김동명 (Dong-Myong Kim)
**펴낸곳** (Publishing Company)_ 도서출판 창조와 지식 (Creation & Knowledge Co., Ltd.)
**디자인** (Book Design)_ (주) 북모아 (Bookmoa Publications Co., Ltd.)
**인쇄처** (Printing Company)_ (주) 북모아 (Bookmoa Publications Co., Ltd.)

**출판등록번호** (Publication Registration Number)_ 제2015-000037호
**주소** (Address)_ 서울 성동구 성수이로18길 31 풍림테크원 1층 103호
  (103, Seongsoo 2 Ro 18-31, Seongdong-ku, Seoul, South Korea)
**전화** (Telephone)_ 070-4010-4856
**팩스** (Fax)_ 02-2275-8577

**ISBN** 979-11-6003-064-8 (03800)

이 책은 저작권법에 따라 보호받는 저작물이므로 무단 전재와 무단 복제를 금지하며,
이 책 내용을 이용하려면 반드시 저작권자와 도서출판 창조와 지식의 서면동의를 받아야 합니다.
잘못된 책은 구입처나 본사에서 바꾸어 드립니다.

The use of any part of this publication reproduced, transmitted in any form or by any means,
electronic, mechanical, photocopying, recording, or otherwise, or stored in a retrieval system,
without the prior written consent of the publisher and the author is an infringement of the copyright law.

Copyright © 2017 by Eun-Jeong Sohn
ALL RIGHTS RESERVED.

지식의 가치를 창조하는 도서출판 창조와 지식
www.mybookmake.com

Authentic Power of Positivity:
There are Only Positive Choices
If You Know Eternity.

# Each Life is
# A BCDE!

## Prologue

I am a 43 year old, Canadian lawyer, who currently works as a partner-level Senior Professional at Yulchon LLC in South Korea, one of the top five law firms with over 400 professionals. Two years ago, I gave birth to my second child and have been on a leave from December 2016 to take care of my children, and I will resign from Yulchon at the end of this year.

Starting from the very beginning, I am the eldest of four siblings of a blind church minister in Daejeon, South Korea. I graduated from Seo Daejeon Girls' High School, majored in Education at Ewha Womans University, obtained an M.A. from the Ontario Institute for Studies in Education (OISE) at the University of Toronto and an LL.B. from the University of British Columbia (UBC). After completion of an articling program in Toronto, I became a lawyer in Ontario, Canada in July 2006. At the time of writing this book, I have worked for more than 10 years as a cross-border transactional lawyer at big law firms in Canada, Singapore and Korea, and am grateful for and pleased with the small achievements that I have made as a professional in this area.

To be clear, the primary reason I am writing this book is not to focus on what I did right to become a lawyer in a competitive environment, having grown up in a medium-sized city in Korea in a modest household with a handicapped father or how I was able to build a successful practice as a woman at big law firms so far. I am fully aware that I have not achieved the ranks of success or reputation that is needed to warrant a right to write a book about an achievement or know-how on success, and I don't hesitate to acknowledge my inadequacy to take on such a task.

At this stage, it should be noted that, while there has been some improvement in recent years, physical handicap, especially blindness, has historically been associated with a strong negative social stigma in Korean culture. Blindness or contact with

## Prologue

blind people was shunned by some in society due to its misled association with bad luck or misfortune.

While it is undeniable that I have focused on my education and career to date, I have also maintained a deep and ongoing interest in how I could encourage the next generation out there who are vulnerable, get easily discouraged, hurt and give up due to a myriad of internal and external reasons, and wanted to send out a message that in some small way help restore their courage and conviction to carry on with their lives in a meaningful and productive way. I had in mind, when writing this book, those who don't even know what to dream, how to survive in this society or how to just live well in the face of so many internal and external challenges and obstacles, such as our own mistakes, failures, unfortunate abusive childhood, any types of mistreatment and/or socio-economic structural barriers like poverty, unemployment, sexism, racism as well as many fateful accidents, injustice and crimes. This book is an English translation of my Korean book with the same title published in October 2017.

Perhaps the most extreme manifestation of discouragement or inclination to give up due to internal or external factors is to take one's life. Unfortunately, Korea has the dubious distinction of having the highest rate of suicide amongst OECD countries as well as in the world. According to Wikipedia[1], about 40 people commit suicide each day, which means on average two people kill themselves each hour in Korea. Isn't it chilling to think that two other human beings voluntarily end their lives in their despair during this very hour that we go on living our own lives… The same source states that about 40% of Korean adolescents have had suicidal thoughts at least once in their lives, and about 10% of them actually tried it in the past. Also, Korea has the highest suicide rate of seniors amongst OECD countries, and 75% of employees suffer from depression according to the survey quoted in this source.

---

[1] https://ko.wikipedia.org/wiki/%EB%8C%80%ED%95%9C%EB%AF%BC%EA%B5%AD%EC%9D%98_%EC%9E%90%EC%82%B4

# Prologue

In principle, I strongly believe that everyone's lives are precious and should be protected and respected and, furthermore, we should have and be given the right to live our lives in the best way possible and in a meaningful, virtuous and productive manner while equally respecting each other's rights. The fact that the weak, the disadvantaged and the vulnerable in our society tend to make this heartbreaking decision to end their lives led me to keep thinking that I should have the courage to send out a message of encouragement based on my experiences and research by publishing a book.

It was back in 2010 when I was working at a UK law firm in Singapore, I sat down to watch a Korean news program which was broadcasted once a week during the weekend in a local TV channel. As usual, I worked a little in the morning, did some chores and sat in front of the TV. On that day, one of the news stories was about the increase in phone fraud. Unexpectedly, the news was delivered in a very personal manner, rather than focusing on the objective statistics. In that news was a summary of one woman's sad life. A young woman who was studying at a small college living alone committed suicide, having lost all the savings her farmer parents saved up and sent to her for college tuition because of phone fraud, and she left a note to say, "I am so sorry, mom and dad." The news piece showed the copy of her note on the screen. On that day, I sat down to just watch the news, but instead this tragic story was broadcast. I was so saddened by her life and that really struck a chord in my heart.

Why was she so weak? Of course, I totally understand why she would be so upset and sorry to her parents knowing how her parents had worked so hard to save up their hard-earned money for her education. However, why did she just choose to end her life based on one wrong decision in her life? Why didn't she take the courage to ask for help around before making such drastic decision? Why wasn't there anybody who could hold her hands and encourage her? Why didn't she have enough self-esteem that could have prevented her from ending her life based on a mere unfortunate incident caused by criminals? With all such swirling

## Prologue

thoughts and questions, I unconsciously decided to go back to Korea to find ways to somehow help young people in Korea who need encouragement now that I have lived, studied and worked overseas more than 12 years. Around the end of 2010, I sent my resume to three big law firms in Korea stating that I am interested in coming back to Korea in the mid- to long- term if there is an opportunity, and Yulchon made an offer requesting me to start immediately. So, after some prolonged thinking and debating with my family, I hurried my plan to leave Singapore to come back to Korea wrapping up the overseas living, and started working as a foreign attorney on January 5, 2011.

My ongoing interest in the importance of encouragement is probably because my father is a handicapped person. I wasn't ashamed of such fact when I was very young, but I began to notice that he was different, and people looked at him at times as time went on. Back in 1970s and 80s, Korea was still heavily prejudiced against the handicapped, and particularly the visually impaired, and they looked down on the blind as unlucky or something to be avoided. Even at such early age, I could sense unkind glances, remarks and treatments growing up at restaurants, in the street or while taking public transportation. I recall, at times, I wanted to scream out to those mean people that, "Do you have any idea how great my dad is despite his blindness?" I felt upset, angry, and sad and at the same time so sorry for my dad for his physical disability because I witnessed how hard it is to live a daily life as a blind man and what an amazing person he is despite such physical challenges. And, while going through such complex emotions and thoughts, I unconsciously became strongly interested in the human mind and how we could hold onto our faith, positive thoughts and conviction despite the uncontrollable environment or unfair socio-economic structural framework so that we could carry on with our lives in the best way possible.

It is true that I tend to easily lose heart or tempted to give up and sabotage myself because I had a father who seemed to be confronted with so many seemingly impossible challenges to live a life as a blind person because even the simplest and smallest

## Prologue

task in our daily lives was like an insurmountable mountain. For example, even in our house, let alone in a new place, he frequently loses direction as to which way is the door, his room or living room because he has to remember in his mind where they are due to his blindness. He frequently bumps into walls or corners and hurts himself, and he does have a lot of scars on his body almost every day of his life. Interestingly, he never shows annoyance or complains upon such injury even when he bleeds or is badly hurt, and he just goes on as if nothing happened. In my mind when I was little, witnessing such incidents so often led me to think that in life there are so many things that you couldn't overcome and there is just nothing you can do about it because everything is just so difficult because my own dad suffers so much with such small daily tasks. Furthermore, I sometimes felt angry at God because He made him suffer like that as a handicapped man even though he was so committed to Him. These conflicting feelings led me to have a somewhat troubled adolescence low in spirit, and I often ended up lashing out and hurting my parents' feelings.

However, after I went to university in Seoul, I started to have so much respect for my parents in the process of maturing as a human being because I have seen the value of their lifestyle, deep-rooted faith and commitment to God, humility and conscientiousness, generosity and forgiveness toward other people, trustworthiness and goodness in them as I continued to have diverse experiences meeting so many different people and going through many trials and errors in my life. They were in fact my perfect role model. My dad, after losing his eyesight in early 20s, became so shaken and despondent to the point of contemplating suicide, but after the drastic conversion from an extremely stubborn atheist to a devout Christian, he has lived a wholly committed life to God and Christian faith ultimately becoming a church minister back in 1980s. He lives each day, completely trusting God, in a very diligent and affirmative manner waking up early in the morning around 2 or 3am, studies bible and meditates, leads a morning service at his church in Daejeon, South Korea at 5am every day and commits himself to the calling and life mission of leading the over 200 church members to the right way of believing based on

## Prologue

the true Gospel of Jesus Christ. Seeing my dad's image from the back always hurrying to the church so that he is never late for any service or appointment and always earlier than on time, carrying the small but quite heavy braille machine that contains the bible and hymns inspires me to the extent of cleansing out the stains of all the complex and somewhat negative feelings and thoughts about the challenges and obstacles in life and prompting me to focus on the importance of faith and commitment no matter what.

In addition, I have grown into a person who strongly believes in the importance of faith in God and positive thinking based on Christian faith and encouragement after having lived in foreign countries for a long time, meeting and working with people from all walks of lives, cultures and religions while reading relevant materials and doing some research consistently for more than 20 years. My primary interest so far has been on how we can take the courage of heart and start again when faced with seemingly insurmountable challenges, hopelessness and obstacles, all sorts of negative feelings like fears, shame, guilt and doubts or low self-esteem due to the unexpected incident, tragedy or ongoing repetitive missteps and shortcomings and yet still continue carrying on with our lives calmly and wisely towards a positive direction. Franklin D. Roosevelt, the 32$^{nd}$ President of the United States who became handicapped at the age of 39 due to a polio and yet courageously and charismatically led the country in the dark periods of the Great Depression and the World War II said that:

> "Courage is not the absence of fear, but rather the assessment that something else is more important than fear."

My life experiences pale in comparison with so many great people in the world who have overcome unbelievable hardships and difficulties, but I determined to write this book for purposes of encouraging those who may benefit from my humble life experiences, accumulated research and readings on subjects related to positive thinking so that they could also decide to take meaningful chances in their lives despite the obvious presence of fear and doubt, with the unprecedentedly courageous mindset as aspired by the President Roosevelt above. I am fully cognizant

# Prologue

of how easy it is to be influenced and swayed by self-destructive thoughts and feelings, hopelessness, negative habits and words, how there are so many socio-economic structural barriers that prevent us from living a meaningful and whole life and how pessimistic and demoralized you can be if you are overwhelmed with the unfairness, injustice and ongoing disasters which are so prevalent in this world. There are so many realistic obstacles and structural problems in society and we may easily be tempted to think that it is no use trying to do better, stay positive or work hard, and it may make more sense just to give up. I am quite familiar with the temptations of such vulnerable feelings and thoughts. On top of that, it is so easy to feel absolutely pessimistic if you think about all the dark forces, abuse, crime, evil people and organizations in this world and the threat to humanity such forces present in our lives. In essence, I have lived my life so far trying to encourage myself or being encouraged by other people despite such forces of darkness and temptation, and this book is an attempt to help those people out there who may share similar doubts, fears, worries and helplessness in the face of deeply entrenched socio-economic structural limitations, various challenges and tragedies in our lives, compounded by our negative feelings and thoughts such as regrets, shame, guilt, fear, anxiety, worries and helplessness and those who, despite all that, still want to live a good life and make a difference towards making a better world.

This book is organized as a few suggestions on how to think and what to do in order to overcome the pattern of negative thinking, not give up and carry on despite such prevalent temptations and risks in our lives, on the basis of my experiences in different countries as well as various books and materials that I came across so far. While it is not a result of an academic research or in-depth study, I dared to make such suggestions because of the interview that I watched a few years ago that Oprah conducted of Rudine Howard. In sum, Rudine suffered from an anorexia nervosa and she was dying from it. When one of the TV celebrities who overcame the disease advised her to "Change your thinking and eat healthy", Rudine responded in such feeble and desperate voice, "I know… but how?" Oprah stated that her question on 'how' had

# Prologue

a profound effect on the direction of her interviews going forward. Rudine was captivated with the erroneous thinking that she was still fat even when she was as thin as 32 pounds and she thought of calories when presented with any kinds of food. She was enslaved by the extreme fear of calories. She wanted to live, and she knew she needed to overcome the illness to survive, but she just didn't know how to overcome her mental illness and screamed out in desperation asking why anybody in the world can't help or teach her find ways to maintain healthy weight and stop thinking that she was fat and let her die like this… She was born in 1964 and died at the age of 32 in 1996. Just before her death, Oprah interviewed her again and asked her whether she had any advice for other teenage girls who suffer from similar illness, and Rudine said, with no strength, "Don't do it…. Save yourself." with tears in her eyes.

Probably all of us know what to do to live a happy life and to overcome when faced with a crisis. It's just so simple and obvious. We just need to take courage and overcome any difficulties. However, when our thoughts and feelings are leaning towards negative direction or it is just realistically impossible to overcome the formidable social barrier, or we are heavily influenced by distorted thinking and incorrect information, then such seemingly simple and obvious advice can't and won't help us. We keep thinking that only we are the victims of such misery, and we are inundated with negative feelings like anger, sadness, loneliness and pain in our heart. In addition, once we are leaning towards that direction, at some point we come to a decision that it is too late to attempt any change and the only thing left to do is to end our life. So, this book consists of a few practical suggestions on new way of thinking and action points that we could take in that time gap between an incident/stimulant and our response to quit it all to make a drastic U-turn in our way of thinking and feeling from negative to positive, based on my life experiences, observations and research in the form of sharing my personal know-how.

> "Between stimulus and response there is a space. In that space is our power to choose our response. In our response lies our growth and our freedom."
> 
> – Viktor E. Frankl

Prologue

As mentioned, I have continuously had a deep interest in the positive mindset in my life and shared my desire to publish a book on this subject to certain people. Some people were quite realistic in that they advised, "Just focus on your life. The woman in the news you saw in Singapore would have committed suicide whether or not there was somebody who could encourage her, and everybody's life is destined. Just because you write a book to encourage others, it's not going to save a person who is destined to die at a particular moment, so just live your life well." In the face of such advice, I always felt ashamed and determined that "Yes, I should just focus on my life and I am not good enough to write a book to encourage others considering that I am not even sure most of the time how to live my life well in this competitive world!" For those people who gave me such advice probably laughed at my desire to help others by publishing a book because I am no celebrity or a modicum of success. Ultimately sharing my personal affairs and details of my family for purposes of encouraging others seem pointless and a dire mistake when I think about how I would regret disclosing my faults, inadequacies and pain with the public.

However, since I was away from work from December 2016, I for the first time in my life have had the time to look back on my life experiences and the people I have met with, and thought about what kind of legacy I wanted to leave in this world at the time of my ultimate departure. While my life is full of mistakes and regrets, I really wanted to leave a legacy that I still worked hard to encourage others, not just close family and friends, and in so doing I wanted to live a fuller, healthier, and more meaningful present life precisely because of such purposeful endeavors in my life. I have made numerous missteps and rushed decisions which later turned out to be disasters, but I intend to open up and share such experiences to argue that we should not sacrifice our present and future because of our misfortune, unexpected incidents, blunders and disappointments in the past. In addition, my present life is not perfect either, but I sincerely hope that sharing my stories may encourage readers to endure current hardships and dream of a better future together.

# Prologue

I truly believe that I was able to come this far mainly because of my loving husband, family, friends and many acquaintances who have encouraged and inspired me whenever I wanted to give up, and as a person who benefitted from such support and most importantly from God's grace, I want to send out this message of hope and encouragement for those who are humble, naïve, and good-hearted and who want to live a good life but who unfortunately stumble and are vulnerable because of various negative feelings and external factors. While I am not qualified to undertake such meaningful mission to write a book with such purpose, I was able to give it a try thanks to the thoughtful and kind support of Mr. Chang Rok Woo, Esq., and Mr. Sai Ree Yun, Esq., the founding partners and Mr. Hee Woong Yoon, Esq., Head of Corporate & Finance at Yulchon LLC. So, I take this opportunity to express my deepest gratitude and respect for their support and leadership.

Last but not least, for me to look back on my life, think about the future directions and ultimately decide to write this book at the crossroad of my life at the age of 43, there indeed was an incident in my life that was beyond my control or understanding by any measurable standards. My sister, Shin Jeong (Sarah) died last July at the age of 39. On that sweltering summer day when we cremated and buried her, I eerily felt so cold and chilly under the burning July sun, and the memory of such contrast makes me feel breathless and the icy coldness overwhelms me and travels from the tips of my fingers through entire body. So, I remind myself to breathe in and out again… I also pray that I may at some point in my life understand God's plan in this unbelievable tragedy and I may restore the warmth of life and overcome the cold darkness captivating myself even under the blazing summer sun.

Looking back, I question whether I even truly loved Sarah as I was frequently upset with her for making things hard for my parents and our family. I never knew what troubled her or what she really needed. In fact, I did not even try to understand her. I was always just too busy to bother, focusing on my life, my problems and my priorities. Sarah suffered from terrible insomnia

# Prologue

and took pills to sleep for a long time. While the circumstances are questionable and sadly there is nothing we can do about that, she died of an accidental overdose and attempted suicide in an extremely feeble state. My heart is still broken, and tears just run down on my cheek whenever I think about her because I could not and did not help her as her older sister. While I am still hurting and lost from her death, it is true that her death served as the main turning point for me to take the courage to finally write this book for purposes of encouraging others by sharing my heartache and life stories. Most importantly, I would like to highlight that the faith in God is the ultimate solution to our pain and suffering for us to regain our courage and hope to step out into the world to live our lives positively rather than hiding in darkness with deep despair and helplessness when faced with seemingly insurmountable challenges and hardships.

I will share my parents' life stories in various sections of this book, but let me briefly introduce my mother here. My mom also suffers from horrible insomnia because she had to do early morning services every day at 5am to help my blind dad as she helped opening up the church doors and turning the lights on and preparing for service. Her insomnia is probably worse than Sarah's because she would usually wake up around 1am and at times she goes to bed around 8 or 9pm and wakes up around 11pm and can't fall asleep again. In such cases, she would just stay awake while most people are sleeping deep into the night. Nonetheless, my mom never took any sleeping pills and never complained or worried about her conditions throughout her life, and rather calmly and peacefully endures her conditions and lives each day joyfully in firm obedience to God's command to rejoice, feeling grateful to God for the brief time of rest, for the rest that other family members are taking, reading bible and singing hymns quietly so that other family members don't awake. She sleeps if she feels sleepy and stays awake if she is not sleepy and she just goes on with her life with such natural flow, ease and gratitude.

While it is just such a simple and obvious proposition, our life is really up to our choices right at this moment. The positivity that is

## Prologue

so crucial in our life is just a willful and intentional choice that we can and should make in contrast to the despair, complaint, blame, resentment or hopelessness that are equally available in front of us, and it is not something that only some of us are born with or something that is so natural that we could just utilize at any given moment without any conscious efforts.

Even in the darkest moments filled with horrible pain and suffering, I firmly believe that we can still live a beautiful and constructive life and achieve supernatural things if we courageously and willfully choose God who has a special plan and purpose for us no matter how unnatural, awkward or impossible it seems to make such a seemingly artificial choice on our end, rather than choosing a natural response to just complain, think and act negatively to such destructive events in our lives.

October 2017<br>Esther Eun-Jeong (EJ) Sohn

# Table of Contents

 Prologue  04

### PART I

## How to think

- 01. Choices  30
- 02. Faith  54
- 03. Thoughts  77
- 04. Pain  90
- 05. True Resilience  103
- 06. My Mistakes Don't Define Me  115
- 07. The Greatest Power: Not Giving Up At This Moment  147

### PART II

## What to do

- 08. Have Faith  162
- 09. Find True Motives  187
- 10. Be Careful with Your Mouth and Heart  201
- 11. Of Course, Work Hard  223
- 12. Respect and Encourage Each Other  229

> Each
> Life is
> .
> .
> A
> Birth
> Choices
> Death
> Eternity!

PART I

# How to think

# 1.
## Choices

**(1) Sheila, The Young Woman I Met during University Years**

I majored in education (with minor in English education) at Ewha and was selected as an exchange student to Thiel College located in Greenville, Pennsylvania, US to study two semesters from September 1996. I chose this college because of the small size as the seniors advised me that it is better to enhance English skills to study at small schools rather than going to a large state university. That was the first opportunity for me to study abroad.

At that time, studying abroad was not that common as it is now, and only about 30 students were selected as exchange students out of about 20,000 students, so it was considered a privilege to study as an exchange student at that time, and I needed to go through a rigorous selection process including evaluation of GPAs and

TOEFL scores and face-to-face interviews. I remember praying to God so hard crying at church that the selection committee somehow selects me, and I was overjoyed when it actually happened. On that summer when I arrived in Greenville in 1996, I was so excited and yet also scared and worried about how I was going to take classes in English and keep an "A" average to maintain academic scholarships going forward. So, a new term started with much excitement and anxiety.

My roommate in the dormitory was a girl named Sheila, who was a bit chubby with curly blonde hair. She was very considerate and quiet and always had a graceful smile on her face. She gave me her high school graduation photo which I still possess and shared her life stories and dreams to become a nurse to make a decent living. She told me that she was adopted and one of her adopted parents was a lawyer and she was very thankful that they sent her to college. She gave me practical advices on American culture and we talked time to time although I was primarily hanging out with other exchange students and spent most of the time at the library to catch up on listening to the recorded lectures and reading assignments.

One day not long after the fall term started, Sheila suddenly became very quiet and frequently stayed in the room all day lying in her bed, which was located across mine in our dorm room covering herself with blankets. I remember her crying quietly at night listening to "You are not alone" by Michael Jackson repetitively which was quite popular around that time. I asked her what the problem was, but she said it was okay and didn't want to talk.

A few days passed and suddenly the dorm superintendent called me into her room and said that, "We are sorry to inform you this and please don't be surprised. Unfortunately, there was a campus accident, and your roommate, Sheila was sexually assaulted by a drunk student at the fraternity party last weekend, and we need to move you to another room as we don't want you to share a room with a student who went through this unfortunate incident as you only spend two terms with us and we really want to ensure that you have the best of the experiences our school has to offer as we cherish the cooperative relationship with Ewha." I was so shocked and didn't know what to do or say, but at any rate, immediately thereafter, I was moved to a room to share it with another exchange student from Japan, and I don't even remember what I said to Sheila at that time.

However, one thing I still remember is my brief encounter with Sheila at one corner of the campus a few months later. I was walking towards a library or classroom that day and on the way, saw her sitting at the steps of one building with other students but she was so drastically different from the time I shared a room together at the beginning of the term. She did not look innocent or like a person who had a dream for her life to be a nurse any more. She was wearing heavy make-up and flashy clothes. I believe she was smoking at that time also.

When our eyes crossed, I said hello and she said hello, and I walked away quickly, but I somehow sensed some sort of nostalgia from her eyes or got a brief glimpse of her graceful smile that I noticed when I first met her. I can't even imagine the horror of a sexual assault to a woman's life and how terrible it is to go through a life with such unfortunate and painful experience, but what I couldn't understand was why her life had to so drastically change because of one negative incident, and I was and am still quite sad and upset to think about that encounter because it didn't seem like her life was progressing toward a positive direction.

## (2) Upward Spiral vs Downward Spiral

Sheila's memory reinforces the mental image that I have on our life trajectory in general. Life comes with many twists and turns. We all go through unexpected incidents in our lives, things don't work out as we expected, and perhaps we regrettably repeat same mistakes. However, our specific response to such internal emotional turmoil and external occurrences leads our life towards the direction of an upward or downward spiral.

The term, "upward spiral" refers to the upward mobility and virtuous cycle of events that lead to positive outcome while the term, "downward spiral" means vicious cycle of events which lead to worsening conditions, series of unfortunate events, failure and one's ultimate destruction. The example of downward spiral is if an unfortunate event happens, we are hurt and upset because of that and we lose heart and depressed, so we don't eat healthy, which in turn results in worsening health and because of the bodily problems and sickness, we become more

"Crisis"

34  How to think

depressed or reach a point of absolute despair. I believe our life is progressing toward the direction of upward or downward spiral specifically due to our choices, and there are three major points I would like to highlight in this regard.

First, just being more fully aware of the fact that our response or choice after the happening of certain negative event or in the face of our continued disappointment with ourselves due to our indiscretions or unfortunate or unfair circumstances will lead our life toward upward or downward spiral may help us make more conscious choice in a positive manner. When faced with such destructive stimulant, it is only natural to respond negatively but, by thinking about the potential consequence, we may be able to hold off such instinctive response and take a more cautious, well-thought out action. Giving ourselves the time and space to think about the effects of the chosen response no matter how trivial it may be, and making ourselves aware of the potential upward or downward implication resulting from the choice would free ourselves from being enslaved by the forces of damaging influences and unhelpful emotions, and exercise ultimate freedom to choose a positive response wisely despite the obvious presence of negative influences and inclinations.

Second, while it may sound somewhat unsympathetic, I believe that negative events or crisis in our life is completely 'neutral' in terms of directing us towards an upward or downward spiral. When you look at the picture above, you notice that the so-called, 'crisis' is located at the exactly same point, and our chosen response determines the direction of upward or downward movement thereafter, but we hastily conclude that any such incident or crisis is in and of itself deleterious and constitutes a force toward a downward spiral only. There are so many inspiring stories and lives that overturned unbelievably unfortunate happenings or problems into miraculous opportunities for supernatural blessings and inspiring outcomes, and that's why there is an expression of "Blessings in Disguise" or "Every cloud has a silver lining", to signify when something bad happens, nobody would argue that it is for the good, but if we handle or overcome it well, we may eventually realize that in fact such happening was not bad at all, and furthermore it was actually beneficial in some respect. That's why the term, "Crisis" in Chinese characters literally means a "Dangerous Opportunity."

The Chief Operating Officer of Facebook, Sheryl Kara Sandberg has had a remarkable career and proven herself an exceptionally talented leader but her personal life is not without a pain. She married at the age of 24 in 1993 and divorced in one year. She met and married her true love, Dave Goldberg in 2004 and had two children, but Dave suddenly died at a resort in Mexico in 2015 running on a treadmill. In one video, she stated that this was the worst experience of her life, and she was in deep despair and sorrow since then. However, she went on to share a story of a turning point when one of her friends advised her to be thankful no matter how hard it is because it could have been worse. Sheryl said that she was so upset and yelled at her friend how he could say such a terrible thing that there could be something worse than losing a love of life like that. At that time, her friend in essence told her that, "Now that we know he had that unknown congenital heart problem all along and he died suddenly but what if he was driving a car with two kids at the back and had the heart attack. He is gone but still left two beautiful kids and that's why I think you should be grateful for them despite the overwhelming sadness." In that video, she acknowledged that she could finally appreciate her friend's advice and found the strength in her heart to go on with her life despite the endless sadness. I saw this video after my sister died, and I think about her story from time to time.

It is quite difficult to be thankful when we are faced with adversity or tragedy in life, but if we can endure the despair and shock with a certain degree of calm in our heart and restore our gratefulness notwithstanding the pain, and conscientiously choose to make positive choices no matter how difficult it is, I believe we can still live a more meaningful and healthy life despite the presence of such undeniable pain and suffering in our heart. The hardship, crisis, difficulty and pain in our life in and of itself does not warrant a downward spiral in our life's direction, and when such incident happens, what is helpful is to remember how our viewpoint, response and choices will lead our lives toward either a constructive upward or destructive downward direction gradually and over time with accelerated speed and added force.

Of course, when something bad happens, human nature seems to suggest that it is only natural to go downward spiral in consideration of the weight of the incident, the pain and heartache and the people's careless views, criticism and words, but let us focus our thoughts and attention on the possibilities that lie in the completely opposite direction. There are so many people who have overcome daily challenges, unbelievable obstacles and torturous treatments and still go on to forgive, move on and walk toward meaning in life, and despite the destructive incident, it is still possible to make a choice toward a constructive upward spiral as long as we are alive.

Third, I want to highlight the importance of freedom from being fixated in one direction even if we made previously indiscreet choices and missteps toward a downward spiral. Even if we had made regrettable decisions in the past, we should be free to always make a new decision and fresh determination to turn around and make a detour toward an upward spiral and in that regard, we should have a flexible mindset believing that our lives are indeed flexible spirals that once a downward spiral can always turn toward an upward spiral at any given point in our lives. We are entitled to change and there are many options and avenues that we could try to make a constructive change and even a transformation. The examples of such positive responses may be meditation, worship, prayer, reading good books including the bible, sharing the predicament with trustworthy friends and family rather than just giving up or making bad choices based on our own lopsided thinking. During that time of careful pondering, we may think about the ways that we could become more wiser and stronger due to the undesirable incident that happened to us and eventually would be able to make a more constructive decision than just reacting immediately and simplistically.

We should have firm conviction that our previously regrettable decisions do not guarantee or predestine our lives toward a downward spiral, and we have our authentic right to choose again and again toward an optimistic direction at any given circumstances. Let us have the flexible mindset that we can alter our life trajectory at any time and let go of our prejudice and self-sabotaging thoughts with a humble heart to look for a different possibility, and one of such possibilities is the willingness to re-direct our mind toward God who has a special plan and purpose for each of us. When we are faced with insurmountable difficulty and challenge, if we think and act affirmatively in reliance of God and His plan for us no matter how unnatural it seems to take such positive viewpoint and action, I believe we can all live our lives to the full extent and, furthermore, in virtuous cycle respecting and encouraging each other with amplified and far-reaching synergy amongst all of us.

## (3) Each Life is A BCDE

I come out with this expression of "Each Life is A BCDE" based on my Christian faith. While internet research indicates that the initial author of the commonly-used expression of "Life is BCD" is arguable, it appears that the French philosopher, Jean-Paul Sartre is the author of the expression that "Life is Choice between Birth and Death." At any rate, this expression using the alphabet is nothing new in that it is widely used in various occasions, and my extension thereon is to include E at the end in the order of the alphabet based on the Christian belief. I strongly believe that each of our lives is truly A BCDE, which are initials of "A Birth, Choice, Death and Eternity", which can be illustrated from the timing standpoint as follows.

Each of Our Lives =

A "Birth"　Many "Choices"　"Death"　"Eternity"
I·····························I············································▶

Each of our lives begins the moment of our respective birth ("B"). There exists a specific plan for us in that God has made such a plan even before we were born, but the tangible form of our existence begins at the time of birth. And almost everything in each of our lives until immediately before our death ("D") depends on our choices ("C"). In addition, as there is eternal life after death to live with God in heaven, I believe our life does not just end at the time of death, and it should continue as eternity ("E"), resulting in the statement that, "Each of Our Lives is A BCDE." Therefore, it should be noted that the assumption, approach and perspective on life is fundamentally different for Christians and non-Christians because the former thinks that the life ends with eternity and the latter death. For Christians, we tend to make seemingly altruistic or sacrificial choices in life simply because we know that there is more to life than just BCD and our decisions are heavily influenced by the weight and significance we impose on the value of eternity throughout our life.

The choices we make each moment have grave significance if we consider the profound effect on our lives in that it determines where we go after death and that period after death is never-ending. Our daily choices have obvious impact on the lifestyle while we are alive, including the small choices such as whether to have breakfast or coffee and what to wear and some big ones relating to our major milestones in our lives like what school we go to, who we choose as friends, who we marry, where we work, which church we go to and which community we belong to. Needless to say, the choices we make when faced with an unexpected accident or crisis are quite significant in shaping our lives thereafter.

At this stage, let us deliberate whether it would be correct to simply believe that our lives end at the time of death and it no longer exists thereafter. I am ashamed to acknowledge this, but I myself often query whether our life is really A BCDE because at times it seems easier and more logical to live a life based on the thinking that life is A BCD only. Eternity just seems so artificial, and I am easily tempted to make choices based on the simple mindset that life is A BCD only, because belief that it is A BCDE makes frequent demands of me to make sacrifice and selfless choices. What a hopeless person I am…In a way, this book is my sincere attempt to breathe in firm belief in myself on how life is indeed A BCDE by making a public statement in the form of publishing a book so that I can truly abide by such a personal belief and share my conviction with people who want to or need to know God and live as a true Christian no matter how challenging it may be.

Ultimately, let us appreciate how each of our lives is so light even when it seems so heavy-ridden with the weight of our concerns and many problems, how it is so simple while it gets so complicated with our doubts and uncertainties at times, how it is so unbelievably short although at times it seems so boring and endless, how it is so very serious while it seems comically obvious, and lastly how it is so inextricably amazing and beautiful while at times it seems so full of pain and suffering all around us.

## (4) About "C"

As mentioned earlier, each of us holds ultimately different perspectives on life as to whether it is A BCD or A BCDE, which guide our choices and lifestyles. My choices would be quite different if I were to believe that life is just A BCD, and this book wouldn't have been published. At any rate, albeit the different conviction on whether there is eternity or not, what seems clear to all of us is that the choices ("C") are of primary importance in our lives. Let me highlight four major points about choices that come to my mind at this stage.

First, the choices include both the small and big ones, and the small choices are equally important as the big ones in constituting and directing each of our lives towards certain direction. There are choices that we make at major milestones in life but small choices that seem so trivial would have lasting impact on our lives as well. So, when we say life is made up of choices, we should not limit them to big ones only and appreciate that even the smallest, tiniest decisions we make are also quite important and meaningful. Even when we are faced with a crisis, a small decision with the courage of our convictions would eventually have a lasting impact on the ultimate outcome no matter how insignificant such small choice seems at the time we make it. In that regard, we should consciously and proactively impose more weight and meaning on our small choices that we make amid any difficulty or challenge. For instance, if you smiled at yourself in the mirror on the day things are not going well to encourage yourself, compliment yourself for your unwavering courage and tenacity. If you chose to hang on your faith and read a book or listen to good music or pray while you were tempted to just resort to self-destructive behaviors like drinking, drugs, or other forms of temporary escape and distraction, encourage yourself for having made such constructive decisions in life despite the appeal of the opposite. When you were able to treat the person who gives you hard time in a kind manner rather than just reacting negatively, be thankful that you have grown into such a mature person. If you went on without giving up, while the lure of just letting go was so resounding, feel proud of yourself at the end of the day and compliment your patience and strong will. And then let us redirect our minds to God trusting His good plans for us and praying for new strength for tomorrow.

Second, while all the big and small choices that we make in our lives are important, no one single choice would be so determinantal in shaping our lives permanently and we have the ultimate freedom to make a completely new choice in a direction that is so opposite to the pattern of the choices we have previously been making in our lives. In other words, the very nature of choices suggests the possibility for change and undeniable flexibility. Our lives in view of an upward or downward spiral does not mean that it is permanently fixed in one direction once we have made certain decisions in our lives in one direction. Rather, what I wanted to emphasize by using such concepts is the flexibility in the direction of our lives based on our simple choices and the power of one tiny decision toward the opposite direction if we had made wrong choices in the past. We should remember that we can always make a U-turn by a small or big decision at any given point in our lives and move toward the upward spiral. That right of ours to make a different choice is our authentic right that no one else can take away from us no matter how controlling that person may be. It is of course quite difficult to make a positive choice when we are so used to making negative ones and there are times in our lives that even a smallest change seems impossible and so foreign considering the forces of the deep-rooted habits and comfort of the familiar. However, if we truly believe that we really need to change the direction of our lives, then we should garner up our courage and determination to make a drastic choice in the opposite direction even if it starts with a tiniest step. Whatever dark force that is giving us challenging time, whatever unfortunate circumstances we are in right now and whatever missteps that we took in the past that we regret so much, nothing in this world can stop us from exercising our authentic right to make a positive choice.

Third, our life presents the potential that it can be bigger, more meaningful and unbelievably influential than the sum of all our choices, big and small combined, and it can be summarized in a simple formula as follows:

$$\text{My Life} \geq \text{My Big Choices} + \text{My Small Choices}$$

This formula suggests two possibilities. First, our lives can be judged to be 'bigger' than the sum of our choices. When we make choices, we may not think about their potential effect in the long run, but in fact some simple choices we make may unexpectedly influence so many people in such a profound way. There is an expression that, "somebody lived larger (or bigger) than life." It may refer to a lifestyle beyond means and conspicuous consumption but sometimes it means that someone had lived and achieved a life that is beyond the ordinary scale, impacting many people in such a meaningful manner. The second possibility is that our lives can be judged to be precisely 'equal' to the sum of our choices. We have lived our life well, making good choices for ourselves, enjoying what life has to offer and no more than that. It could be a life well-lived based on smart choices and calculated risks and decisions or it could be a short-lived life with a decision to end voluntarily, but at any rate, that is just it.

However, we all know that ultimately we do not live in isolation. We live our lives in this world with the desire to be and live bigger than ourselves at some point exerting a positive influence on other people beyond our own. Once we have achieved something, we have the inherent desire to help others and make meaning out of our achievement in doing so. We want to be understood by people about what we stood for and what we believed in, and we want to go beyond just enjoying what we have and share our joy and fulfillment with others. I believe if we can make choices based on such good intention to help others and have positive influence on others, then the perimeter of our influences is boundless, and it could help many people in the world ultimately making the place we live a much better one. So let us use our right to choose in a wise, patient, positive and careful manner bearing in mind the profound potential of the upward spiral trying to live our lives larger than the sums of each choice, appreciating the flexibility and possibility that we are free to make a different choice than the ones before turning towards a positive direction at any point in time, believing that even the smallest and seemingly insignificant choice today will have a substantial impact on the overall direction of our lives, and ultimately knowing that the right to choose is our own authentic right that no one else can take away from us even in the worst moment of our lives.

Fourth, if we truly believe that each of our lives is A BCDE, our choices cannot be of a negative, skeptical or selfish nature. I dare to argue that "If we truly know E, then there is no negative C and there are only positive Cs." By 'truly knowing,' I include 'believing in it' as well. When we fully appreciate and believe in the concept and promise of eternity as stated in the bible, we can eliminate lots of damaging and undesirable choices that we make, enslaved by greed, obsession, unhelpful emotions and flawed thinking, and instead live a life led by God and His Spirit helping others and sharing His good news. In my case, it's always when I lose faith or doubt the existence of eternity that I make regrettable choices driven by discouraging thoughts and negative emotions like anger, sadness or disappointment resulting from various incidents in life, without even thinking about my authentic right to choose otherwise despite such overwhelming influence. Interestingly, the bible explains that the concept of the eternity is a "secret".

> "He replied, because the knowledge of the secrets of the kingdom of heaven has been given to you, but not to them. Whoever has will be given more, and they will have an abundance. Whoever does not have, even what they have will be taken from them." (Matthew 13:11-12)

The secrets are unfair in that only those who get it will get it, and those who are not supposed to know will never know. The creator of the secret decides to whom it will be known and to whom it will remain as a secret forever. Therefore, those who are not supposed to know it will consider the concept of heaven and eternity as a silly proposition that is irrelevant to their lives or it's just a waste of time and energy to even think about it. One has to wonder, if that's the case, why did God make it a secret? In my view, I believe the fact that the concept of eternity being a secret in and of itself signifies that it is the essence of the message of hope, encouragement, pre-destination and salvation towards those He loves and selected in order that we are inspired and encouraged to 'never' give up in the face of any unbearable forces of darkness, challenge or hardship because there is such a mysterious and enigmatic secret to eternal life that we will enjoy at the end of our miserable and heartbreaking physical lives that other people would never realize.

I know it is so easy to doubt eternity because I also lose perspective at times, living a busy life of a competitive lawyer. My parents deeply worry whenever I express my skepticism and I feel bad for causing such worry when I discuss this issue with them.

However, deep in my heart, I am fully in agreement that God has planted me in my family so that I can have the conviction in Him and eternity based on my knowing, watching and witnessing how my parents have lived their lives based on strong faith and absolute commitment all their lives. In other words, my birth in my family itself is to me evidence that God had a plan to save me out of my stubborn disbelief and doubts. And I always remind myself to remember His plan, grace and goodness in having done so to deliver me from the forces of darkness, doubts and skepticism that tempt me in so many respects and to follow Jesus in all ways of my life with a grateful heart. In a sense, this book is an open declaration of my faith and conviction so that I can reinforce myself toward the path of strong commitment to God and eternal life no matter how embarrassing it is to publicly confess my occasional doubts and disbeliefs and also a sincere attempt to help and encourage others as well as myself to not lose heart or faith in any difficulty or despair and, most importantly, to choose God no matter what.

It is indeed a 'mystery' to stay positive and make affirmative choices based on the conviction of eternity to those who are not aware of the secret of eternity. So, remembering that the bible stated the concept of eternity and heaven as a secret, let us build our lives, based on the deep assurance of such secret and power no matter how difficult the situation we are in now may be, and have the courage to continue to make positive and meaningful choices for us as well as others. The proclamation that "Each of our lives is A BCDE" is therefore a statement that underscores the infinite hope and possibility even to the lives that are so heavily and deeply damaged and destroyed by the forces of darkness, human errors and problems where neither the best of positive psychology nor self-help mechanism can help due to the severity of hurt and despair, because only with God who created the universe and each of us with His own words, exists such everlasting hope and unimaginable possibility to fundamentally change, heal, and restore our lives. So, let us choose faith and eternity that is the truly unshakable and formidable foundation of any positive mindset and go on with our lives making small and big choices toward true happiness, love, freedom and hope as promised by the Almighty God.

# 2.
# Faith

### (1) Where Does the Help Come From

I want to share an experience that helped me appreciate where the true help comes from. Singapore is an island, city state in Southeast Asia, so meticulously organized and maintained by the government. Many corporate offices of multinational companies are located in the high-rise buildings concentrated in an area called Raffles Place and I worked in there from 2006 until early January 2011. It was one of those scorching summer days back in 2008 and I recall my office was located on the 28$^{th}$ floor at that time. I sometimes looked out just to relax my eyes from continuously working on the computer, and that day when I looked out, there was something strange that I had never seen before that caught my eyes. A box-shaped container was hanging close to the top of the high-rise building right across ours, and it just seemed so strange at that time because the purpose of it was not clear at all. It wasn't a cleaning tool and it didn't seem like it was trying to move something either. It just hung there for some time somewhat precariously, being swayed by winds occasionally at times.

Some time passed, and suddenly, out of the blue, I started thinking that the then-current condition of that thing was so similar to our common human destiny in a sense that we all try so hard to hang on to our achievement and that we work so hard to move up the corporate ladder, assuming that thing must have moved up from the ground floor to the close to the top floor, and while we may have achieved some degree of success and height in social stature, we are in essence so vulnerable and precarious due to the ongoing and exacerbating competition all around us. And once that thought came into my mind, I suddenly started to have increased concern about that thing in that I worried what might happen to it if it suddenly falls because of some fault in the line that's holding it, if there is a person inside, and if the wind becomes stronger than now and cause it to sway further and end up crashing. Interestingly, occasional observation of that container outside the window while continuously working gave me some sort of artificial excitement and anxiety because I imposed such meaning and color to that mere object hanging by the building up there. My only concern was that it should come down safely to the ground floor without an accident as that would be the safest place for that container to go back to the starting point.

But suddenly that container was abruptly pulled from the above and sat on the top of that high-rise building as if nothing happened. It happened so fast and compared to the previously precarious status where it was just hanging by the window being swayed by wind left and right, that container was so secure and settled on the top of that building across ours and I unconsciously exclaimed "Wow!" when I saw it happen. Looking back, perhaps it was not an exceptional or notable in that it was just waiting to be pulled up to the top floor after some time and this was not an uncommon occurrence, but for whatever reason it was just an exciting moment when that thing went up suddenly, forcefully pulled up onto the roof, rather than going down to the ground floor as I anticipated all along.

The reason that this small incident became a noteworthy event to me is because it taught me of my ignorance and limitations of my biased thinking. First of all, I was ignorant. I didn't even know what that was, where it belonged, and whether it was already meant to be positioned on top of that building (because it was attached to the crane that would make it so), and due to that ignorance, I kept worrying about how it would safely come down to the ground floor. Second, I held such a prejudicial viewpoint in that I had no idea that the solution to that situation was the crane on the roof that was securely holding that container, and was fixated on the idea that it should be brought down to the ground floor. In other words, the solution that I focused on was completely opposite to the correct answer to the problem, and I was entirely wrong in that regard. What fascinated me about that incident is that my thinking evolved in one direction only – i.e., how it can come down safely because it seemed dangerous to be hanging there. However, all my anxiety, worries and wishes were in a sense a waste of my time and energy because it was just simply wrong. The correct answer was in the opposite direction. It is somewhat embarrassing that I could not think of the other possibility that the container could be pulled up, but it was quizzical how my thinking was so fixated in one direction that turned out to be totally incorrect. In the end, as the container was close to the top of that building, that solution was indeed the best one and perhaps some people may have already known that answer as soon as they saw it, but for whatever reason I associated that image with our efforts to be successful and to go to the top and considering the hardships and efforts to come up to that height, all I wanted was to go down and rest on the ground floor. In a sense I was captivated by my prejudice and lopsided thinking in looking at that situation and did not even realize that I was so far from the right solution to that problem.

At that very moment when the container was pulled up so suddenly, I realized that I could actually be quite silly in some fundamental level if I am so absorbed in my prejudice and one directional thinking. In a way, the more I think in one direction, the further I could be pulled away from the ideal solution to a problem. So, I always think of that incident when I am so confident that I am 100% right in certain situations to open up the possibility that perhaps I am wrong and there is a different way to look at the problem from the opposite direction. And I remind myself that I should free myself from the erroneous thinking or lopsided prejudice that is holding me in despair, worries, fear and anxiety and do my best to maintain humility and optimism in view of all sorts of possibilities in the universe.

On top of that realization, this incident helped me to strengthen my faith in God to fully appreciate that the true help to aid any given situation comes from the "above", rather than "down below" as it was the case for that crane that pulled firmly and abruptly from the above in an instant without any hesitation. I want to share the bible verses that my mother likes, and I also appreciate:

> "I lift up my eyes to the mountains – where does my help come from? My help comes from the Lord, the maker of heaven and earth." (Psalm 121:1-2)

Whenever I complain about the difficulties and challenges in life, my mom quietly listens to me and sometimes whispers to me in a quiet voice, "Have you seen the mountain lately? You know where the help comes from, right?..." And then she turns her eyes back to the bible that she was reading.

Nobody in this world can survive or truly live a meaningful life all by oneself. We all need help from others. We have lived because of someone else's help so far and we should help others as we have been helped. If I am an adult with an able body, it means that somebody took care of me when I was just an infant who could not even sit up straight and eat any solid food. If I can read, it means that somebody took the time and efforts to teach me how to read and write. Malcolm Gladwell wrote the book, "Outliers: The Story of Success" highlighting how in every success story where the hero or heroine may argue that he or she did it all by himself or herself, they still benefitted from the care and help of others such as family, friends and community, certain unique opportunities presented to them particularly because of the time and circumstances that they were born, and certain system of belief or culture that they were part of at the time of their upbringing. Why don't we let go of the faulty thinking that "I can do it all by myself and I don't need anybody's help and if things don't work out, I will just give up and end my life", and instead choose courage, openness and generosity to seek help from others and after attaining a certain status in society then I will go on and be the person who help others and shed light in this dark world? And the best helping hands that we can resort to in this world is the most trustworthy, powerful and everlasting helping hands of our Savior, God who created the universe and is still working right at this moment for our benefit and for our true deliverance.

## (2) Deliverance vs Self-Deliverance (Suicide)

Christianity is based on God's salvation, which is a fundamentally critical element that distinguishes it from other religions. The salvation denotes how God graciously saved our destiny from the lives of hopeless sinners to the children of God only if we believe in Jesus who came to save us and restore our relationship with God due to our sinful nature that was inherited from Adam and Eve. We were destined to live based on our greed, prejudice, pride, pleasure and bodily desires but because we believe in Jesus Christ, we are reborn as a 'new creation' that is so fundamentally different from our old selves and are granted with a completely new opportunity to live a new life full of faith and hope for the future and eternity as the children of the Almighty God. This is an exceptional upward mobility in our status from the sinner to the child of God and that possibility of fundamental transformation exists only if we believe in Jesus, and that's why the message of salvation and deliverance is good news, the Gospel.

In life, being granted a second chance is such an amazing gift, as it is so rare and hard to have a genuine second chance in a ruined relationship or damaged reputation. For example, once we fail an examination, it is most likely that the failure remains unless we incur additional efforts and costs to re-take that exam again. Likewise, at work if we made certain mistakes, it is most likely that we are stuck with the stigma in that area unless we put a lot of efforts into overcoming that overwhelming prejudice and reputation. But the Almighty God grants us with the opportunity to have a fresh start and have a second chance freely without any efforts or costs on our end by upgrading our status from the doomed sinner to the child of God only if we believe in Jesus Christ as our Savior. Even after our rebirth, God continuously encourages and gives another chance whenever we tumble and fall throughout our lives.

What was truly illuminating to me was the fact that while the term, 'salvation' is synonymous with redemption and 'deliverance', 'suicide' is the same as 'self-deliverance.'

> "Trust in the Lord with all your heart and lean not on your own understanding." (Proverbs 3:5)

This passage from the bible always reminds me to turn back from negative thoughts and despair, and instead rely on the message of hope, wisdom and love as contained in the bible whenever my thoughts are turning towards a detrimental direction. When something bad happens unexpectedly, the natural response is to question, "Why me?" and we may feel engulfed by the anguish and sadness when our eyes are fixated on the problem, rather than the ray of light that exists at the end of the dark tunnel. In the midst of the darkest tunnel when we refuse to look further to find the light at the end, we make the deliberate decision to end our lives because the only thing we could do to save ourselves from the impending misery seemed to be to just end it for good, and I believe that's why the suicide is called self-deliverance. But ending one's life is not a true deliverance no matter how difficult the life is at that particular moment, and, to be saved, we should seek help, think differently and try various options and ultimately rely on the helping hands of Almighty God who already knows the hardships we are facing and the beautiful plan that is ahead of us only if we hold onto faith and hope in God. Ending one's life does not result in any positive outcome and it can't benefit anybody while holding on to faith and overcoming seemingly impossible challenges always gives hope and inspires so many people. Let us not choose the tragic, cruel self-deliverance, but rather choose true deliverance rendered by God who created this universe, refusing to listen to the lures of the dark force using poisonous emotions like regret, guilt, loneliness, pain, fear, doubt and disappointment that lead to the downward spiral, and instead proactively choosing to hold onto the firm hands of the Almighty God who is pulling us forcefully from the above for the true deliverance from all our predicaments.

A few years ago, I saw the interview of my dad on the CTS program "Rejoicing Night and Day" and his answer to the question of the interviewer, "Who is God from your experiences so far?" My dad responded that, "God in my mind is a big helping hand." Initially, I thought that "Oh that's just so simple. I wish he answered in a more elaborate, sophisticated manner!" But, once I heard his explanation, I understood what he meant… He explained that God came to him first when he collapsed and fell on the ground out of despair and misery due to the sudden blindness that happened in early 20s, and He offered His graceful helping hands to save him from the valley of deep anguish and sorrow without any hope for the future when he was giving up on himself trying to even commit suicide at some point. His hands are so big in that He generously invites those who are unwilling, disbelieving and rebellious against God with open hearts and a graceful embrace.

Why don't we take the courage to grab His generous and gracious hands offering help and ultimate deliverance so that we can get out of the pit of misery and pain. Why don't we trust His hands instead of resorting to people's hands who extend their help only when it is convenient or beneficial to them? Why don't we live our lives holding His hands, never letting go of our faith in Him that lead us to heaven after our death to continue with our lives in such a beautiful place where there is no tears and no suffering.

## (3) Limits of Self-Help

There are a lot of systems of positive psychology and research on self-help mechanism as well as numerous institutions, think-tanks, organizations and companies which focus on positivism, mind-control, wellbeing and spirituality. I acknowledge that to a certain extent those system and mechanism do work, and we need their help at times. However, such system and efforts have a fundamental weakness in that in the worst possible moment when we don't even have the heart or willingness to go on, it just can't help. It is somewhat ironic to think about this problem because while those secular means can help us to a certain extent, its usefulness pales and perishes in the worst possible moment when we are faced with extreme self-hatred, lethargy, fear, anxiety, sense of loss and despair reaching out to suicidal thoughts out of desperation. It just ends up becoming a nuisance or annoyance just because our mind doesn't even want to hear about it due to a lack of will and hope to go on any longer. It is at that moment that we realize it is ultimately only one source that we can rely on in the worst-case scenario that exists beyond the realm of our physical will and desire, which is the Almighty God who promises us unlimited hope and love that is possible in our lives through His love and amazing grace. Therefore, we should have the wisdom and courage of conviction to choose God above all else, no matter how tempting and persuasive the other alternatives appear.

## (4) Universe: The Ratio of Light and Darkness

When we watch news on TV or other social media outlets, there are so many unbelievably cruel things that are happening in this world such as crimes against humanity, torture, injustice and abuse let alone war, disaster and genocide, and it is very easy to think that there is no God and it is more logical to just live as an atheist, rather than a believer because if there is God, there should not be such pain and suffering in the world. I am quite susceptible to such disbelief because I feel so upset when especially horrible things happen to the weak and vulnerable in our society such as children, women and the handicapped, and I would cry out to God why He would let these things happen even though He has the power to stop it all. It is so easy to blame structural issues, economic inequality and social injustice and people who misuse their power when things look so hopeless and dire. I also fall into the lure of thinking that perhaps religion is just an artificial belief system that was created by some people to manipulate others into false hope or faith and/or take advantage of others.

That's the reason that I am so grateful to God that He has sent me to be the eldest daughter of my parents so that I can witness their life-long devotion and commitment to God; hence, inevitably I become a devoted Christian myself. I did have a somewhat troubled adolescence because I was ashamed of having a handicapped father and I felt upset about God because He made my dad blind and suffer for the rest of his life, but once I became more mature, I finally realized that it was all part of God's plan and love to save him as well as myself.

In Korea, there is an expression that, "The value of eyesight is 90% of the whole body," and eyesight is that important in our life. My dad was a stubborn atheist who refused the concept of God until he became blind at the age of 20. Through such crisis, he and my grandparents resorted to so many ways to treat the disease, including various well-known doctors and different religions and in the end, he heard a mysterious voice compelling him to "Go home and go to church" when he was doing a temple stay in remote mountain because my grandparents wanted him to commit to Buddhism. Since he heard that enigmatic voice, he turned away from disbelief to God and lived a life of devotion which led him to be a pastor eventually. I have seen his ways of living and I can absolutely testify that I could never be a Christian without having witnessed his life and his commitment. I am quite full of doubts and skepticism and analytical and I tend to think over and over and all these characteristics would definitely lead me to be a non-believer, rather than a believer. Also, I am somewhat pessimistic because I see that there is so much darkness in the world, and when I see my dad bumping into corners of our own house injuring himself so often because he can't see the obstacles or things in front of him, I feel so much pain in my heart and at times get resentful. But I know for a fact that my dad completely transcended his physical limitation and agony, and he is simply too happy to feel sorry for himself because God is his Savior and He is his Lord to lead him to the eternal home after the end of this journey in this life. His hope in Jesus and the Lord enables him to deal with the daily challenges in an absolutely positive manner and he is much more optimistic than myself in many respects and I am so inspired in so many respects just watching him and listening to his sermon.

I completely understand the atheists. When I was working at UK law firms, one of the British partners asked me one day, "You are a lawyer and how could you be a Christian at the same time?" He was genuinely curious about how someone who is trained to think logically could be a believer of heaven and the message of the Gospel. His viewpoint is that if you have a brain to think logically and are smart to a certain extent, the Christian theology is just too illogical to believe. While part of me was in some way envious of him, I felt sorry for him. For one, I was envious of his confidence that as long as you have some thinking brain, you should have such confidence to throw out any belief system that could sustain you. You basically don't need anything else other that yourself! But more importantly, I felt sorry for him because his smart brain is preventing him from knowing the true savior of our life who can fundamentally transform our existence and rejoice in the amazing love and grace, and his smartness is in some fundamental way a flawed thinking that we don't need God when in fact we can't do anything at all without the help of the Almighty God.

When I am faced with all the terrible events in the world as broadcast in the news or when I witness or experience social injustice and economic inequality, it is so easy to lose faith and choose hopelessness. However, whenever that kind of darkness overwhelms me, I always think about how God's first creation was the light when he saw the darkness in the universe in the book of Genesis, and how God has commanded that we Christians should live our lives as the light in this world. For whatever reason, the image of endless darkness that dominates the universe and the rarity of the bright light reminds me of the power of true light that can only be found through God and why it is so hard to find and to be that force of light in this world that is full of darkness and how God is still shedding the light for me to enlighten me out of the ignorance and doubts so that I can be led to the path of salvation, rather than staying in the valley of shadow and death. Ultimately, I remember how I could not do anything at all without the power of the light that is in Jesus Christ alone.

> "God said, "Let there be light" and there was light."
>
> (Genesis 1:3)

We all know how expansive the universe is and the following is a brief description of the immeasurable size of the universe:

> "The size of the Universe is somewhat difficult to define. According to a restrictive definition, the Universe is everything within our connected spacetime that could have a chance to interact with us and vice versa. According to the general theory of relativity, some regions of space may never interact with ours even in the lifetime of the Universe due to the finite speed of light and the ongoing expansion of space. For example, radio messages sent from Earth may never reach some regions of space, even if the Universe were to exist forever: space may expand faster than light can traverse it. Distant regions of space are assumed to exist and to be part of reality as much as we are, even though we can never interact with them. The spatial region that we can affect and be affected by is the

observable universe. The observable universe depends on the location of the observer. By traveling, an observer can come into contact with a greater region of spacetime than an observer who remains still. Nevertheless, even the most rapid traveler will not be able to interact with all of space. Typically, the observable universe is taken to mean the portion of the Universe that is observable from our vantage point in the Milky Way. The proper distance-the distance as would be measured at a specific time, including the present-between Earth and the edge of the observable universe is 46 billion light-years (14 billion parsecs), making the diameter of the observable universe about 91 billion light-years ($28×10^9$ pc). The distance the light from the edge of the observable universe has travelled is very close to the age of the Universe times the speed of light, 13.8 billion light-years ($4.2×10^9$ pc), but this does not represent the distance at any given time because the edge of the observable universe and the Earth have since moved further apart… Because we cannot observe space beyond the edge of the observable universe, it is unknown whether the size of the Universe is finite or infinite." (Wikipedia[2])

---

[2] https://en.wikipedia.org/wiki/Universe#Size_and_regions

But what impresses me the most about this infinite, almost immeasurable universe is that it is full of dark energy and dark matter, which constitutes approximately 96% of the universe, and the proportion of the light is around slightly more than 4% and less than 5% in total as follows:

> "More is unknown than is known. We know how much dark energy there is because we know how it affects the universe's expansion. Other than that, it is a complete mystery. But it is an important mystery. It turns out that roughly 68% of the universe is dark energy. Dark matter makes up about 27%. The rest - everything on Earth, everything ever observed with all of our instruments, all normal matter - adds up to less than 5% of the universe. Come to think of it, maybe it shouldn't be called "normal" matter at all, since it is such a small fraction of the universe." (NASA[3])

I find this research available on internet so intriguing. I probably knew all along that the universe is full of darkness and the lights are numerous but quite underwhelming in comparison with the vast darkness. However, the fact that the ratio of dark and light is so incomparable to the extent of 96:4 or 95:5 seems to suggest an

---

3) https://science.nasa.gov/astrophysics/focus-areas/what-is-dark-energy

inspiring point in relation to God's command that we should be living our lives as light in this world.

> "You are the light of the world. A town built on a hill cannot be hidden. Neither do people light a lamp and put it under a bowl. Instead they put it on its stand, and it gives light to everyone in the house. In the same way, let your light shine before others, that they may see your good deeds and glorify your Father in heaven." (Matthew 5:13-16)

The bible clearly dictates that we believers should be the light of the world as above. However, in the universe there is only about 4% of light and whenever I feel despair, upset and full of doubt about God, I keep thinking about this ratio, and appreciate that it is no surprise that I easily lose faith because the world is so full of disbelief and dark force. Therefore, I choose hope and faith in God, instead of getting absorbed into the darkness, despair, doubt and skepticism and make a fresh resolution to live a truly devoted Christian life no matter how challenging it may be.

In particular, the prevalence of darkness in this world is augmented when we notice that even those who call themselves as Christians live and act even worse than non-believers making more selfish decisions taking advantage of others, justifying their wrongdoings using the bible and hurting others within the church and the community. When we look at those incidents, we easily lose perspective and faith in God for want of any living examples that truly follow Jesus Christ in a wholistic manner.

In Korea, there is an expression that "There are more non-believers inside the church than outside." Considering the overwhelming numbers of Christians and mega churches in Korea, such expression is quite mind-blowing and something we need to deeply reflect upon. Without humble reflection and deep introspection, I don't think there is a chance to make a fundamental change in ourselves to redirect our minds from the selfish desires to the holy ones and good intentions based on the true conviction on God and eternal life.

However, even in such dire circumstances, let us remember that it is part of the reality that constitutes 96% of the physical world and it is really not necessary to feel disappointed, hurt, upset or angry and we should just calmly resort to the quiet calling of Jesus Christ and commit to Him no matter what. It is that rarity that makes it so valuable to find the true faith and ultimate salvation, and as we were once all part of darkness, it is of course so easy to feel comfortable being in that state of darkness, but the inevitable truth is that only the force of light is the weapon against the dominant power of darkness in this world and that is the fundamental reason that we should always look to the light, instead of lamenting the prevalence of darkness in this world to live the life of the light as directed by God.

# 3. Thoughts

## (1) Think again!

When we are absorbed in one frame of thought and our perspective is limited by our prejudicial thinking that there is no hope in this world, it is really impossible to find a glimpse of hope in this world because our thoughts lead our words and actions. I wrote a Master's Thesis on "Women's Underemployment in South Korea: A Conceptual Framework and Preliminary Analysis" back in 2002 at OISE, University of Toronto focusing on female underemployment as a result of unfair global economic structure. When you are not happy with the status quo of this world and there does not seem any practical solution to such inherent structural problems, the easiest thing to do is to complain and criticize, to lose heart, and to get angry and mistrust the authority and the system in general.

However, the unbearable darkness can only be resolved by the light. And, we need to take courage to shine the light amid darkness to overcome such force, instead of focusing on the problem of darkness. When we are possessed with negative thinking and worries, we should have the maturity to look beyond and accept with humility that the way we think may not be the right solution to the impending problems. As I shared in the earlier section, I unfortunately kept thinking that the only solution for that container hanging by the high-rise building was for it to come down to the ground floor safely, but the correct solution was to pull it up to the top floor to overcome that precarious circumstance. Thanks to that small incident, I now know that it is possible that the solution I have in mind could be completely wrong and particularly if my thought is leaning towards undesirable direction or is losing its balance in perspective, and I quickly resolve to "Think again!" in a completely different direction and open my mind to a whole new possibility.

Some years ago, I had a misunderstanding with a junior lawyer in the same team, so I invited her for an informal chat for purposes of resolving the issue by having an open discussion. I truly believed in the power of communication, and I was confident that we could resolve any issues as long as we speak openly and honestly with each other. She graduated from a top university in Korea and she passed the bar with a top score and seemed to be so smart and capable. Regarding the particular incident that we had a difference of opinion, I first shared my views in the hope that she could see where I come from and then funny thing happened. She started talking about something entirely irrelevant to that incident and she was so utterly focused on that issue while clearly exhibiting to me she did not even bother to listen to or care what I had just said. That other factor she raised was not an objective event that happened, and it was a false assumption made out of her own prejudice based on an experience that she had with someone else in the past, but she somehow could not get over that particular viewpoint in relation to our issue. It is at that moment I felt almost for the first time in my life that I was talking to a formidable wall that was not interested in hearing me, and I understood what it meant to have difficulty in communication with some people.

Until that point in time, I had never experienced any significant communication issues with work colleagues, but the experience with her taught me that sometimes it just doesn't work. The thought of suicide is an attempt to deliver oneself out of the imminent hardship, instead of listening to others or opening oneself to different possibilities to resolve the issue at hands. It is of course possible to at least think about it at times if the reality is just so hard to live with, and considering that there are so many obstacles and challenges in this world, the temptation of wanting to end one's life when things don't work out as expected is quite understandable. That is why it is so important that we have the flexible mind to acknowledge that the negative thinking that I am possessed with right now may not be the right way of thinking and there are other ways to look at the situation and to consciously redirect ourselves towards a different direction. Also, we should have the courage to seek help from others to the extent necessary by turning to some trustworthy friends, family members, schools, churches and other various organizations and institutions.

Those who are so absorbed in their own thoughts are like those who are imprisoned. They don't communicate with outside people and they are isolated in their own thoughts believing that only theirs is right. Even if our physical life is unfortunately similar to such imprisonment, we need to remember that no matter where we are and no matter how our liberty is limited, we have the authentic freedom, right and power to make a choice as to how we think about our current condition and how we will move forward. So, let us think again in a positive direction, raising fresh questions on our assumptions and unwarranted expectations and finding ways to recover from our own mistakes and wrongdoings, doing our best to find ways to do things differently than before for the ultimate goodness when things look impossible and instead of trying to do it all by oneself, asking for help and working together with others to make something meaningful and beautiful out of a seemingly hopeless situation. Like Sheryl Sandberg, let us look for ways to think differently about the current incident and misfortune. Such an attempt to think differently and positively may appear quite unnatural, awkward, or artificial particularly because a negative response seems most natural to the destructive event in our lives, but I truly believe that an extraordinary outcome is possible only when we choose to think and act in the positive direction no matter how difficult it may be, resorting to a firm faith in the Almighty God who is in control of this vast universe.

## (2) Don't take it personally

When we are discouraged or disappointed by something bad that happened, people frequently advise, "Don't take it personally." This expression means that while it is unfortunate, it is not because of who we are or what we've done and it's just an accident and we should get over it. Of course, it is hard to easily let go of resentment and disappointment when things don't turn out as expected, but we are all warriors in each of our lives, and some people are good, and some are not, some are courageous, and some are mean, some intentionally hurt others because they were hurt while some try to help others despite their own pain and suffering because they have a gracious heart.

Therefore, perhaps we unfortunately got injured because we happened to be tied with someone not so desirable during our lives or maybe someone intentionally try to hurt us, but we should not take it so personally to the extent that that incident would be the sole determinant of our future direction of our lives, and we should appreciate the possibility that despite that we should overcome and move forward with a graceful heart.

Furthermore, let us look at the negative incident or crisis in a neutral way to the extent possible because we know for a fact that so many heroes and heroines were once faced with such unbelievable challenges and hardships, that they overcame to achieve something so meaningful and beautiful and continue to inspire all of us towards the path of greatness. When something bad happens, the most important thing is to think about how to respond to such negative event in our lives in the most positive way possible given the circumstances. Of course it is unfair and unjust and it is upsetting that something bad happened, and there are so many structural restraints in our society that prevent us from living our lives to the fullest, but as long as we are fixated with the problem, darkness and negative circumstance instead of turning our attention to the light and ultimate salvation, building a formidable wall of isolation to distance ourselves from the outside world, there would not be any chance for the powerful force of light to shine into the darkness that is so prevalent in this situation and the status quo would never change for the better.

## (3) Bumble Bee

During my university years, I read an article about a bumble bee. Aerodynamically, it is impossible that it flies because the body is too big for the size of the wing and one internet source explains as follows:

> "Short and stubby, the bumblebee doesn't look very flight-worthy. Indeed, in the 1930s, French entomologist August Magnan even noted that the insect's flight is actually impossible, a notion that has stuck in popular consciousness since then. Now, you don't need to be a scientist to raise an eyebrow at this assertion, but it sure is easier to explain the bumblebee's physics-defying aerodynamics if you're Michael Dickinson, a professor of biology and insect flight expert at the University of Washington. "The whole question of how these little wings generate enough force to keep the insect in the air is resolved," Dickinson told Life's Little Mysteries. "There are details remaining, but it's just not an enigma anymore."" (Live Science[4])

---

4) https://www.livescience.com/33075-how-bees-fly.html

The bumble bees, not knowing the scientific basis for their inability to fly, fly around diligently collecting honey and nectar to sustain their livelihood.

I encourage us to remember the image of this bumble bee when we are faced with seemingly impossible challenges in our lives. If we keep focusing on why it won't work out, why it's not possible and why it is better to just give up, we will never be able to achieve anything in life. It seems so natural to just give up and it seems impossible to think otherwise as the reality seems so hopeless at times. Based on such a pattern of thinking, we are unavoidably directed to make small and big negative choices leading our lives to the downward spiral toward the ultimate demise into the darkness. If we focus on the impossibility, only the impossible reasons will show, and if we turn our eyes toward the possibility, we will be able to find ways to still make it possible and move forward. Just like the bumble bee, we should move beyond the once popular and authoritative diagnosis that "it is impossible" and take the courage to just try and do it despite the obvious challenges and I truly believe that something meaningful can and will be achieved.

## (4) When Your Survival is Threatened, Think Thrive

The easiest thing to do when faced with adversity is to complain, give up and despair. It is so natural and expedient, but there is no benefit from such an expected reaction. However, if one takes the courage to overcome the difficulties and hardships, then the resulting possibilities are limitless, and it is beneficial not only to the person but also to so many people out there who will be inspired by such courage and achievement. We can find inspiration in the story of Khadijah Williams who lived a homeless life from when she was six years old and she, together with her mother and sister, stayed at the Los Angeles' Union Rescue Mission's Refugee for Homeless Families. However, instead of complaining about her life, she focused on her studies and always did homework and continued to read until 10 pm when the lights in the facility were automatically turned off. For over 10 years, she continued to live like that and if she could not get a space in that temporary shelter, she slept over at bus or train stations or on the street. Ultimately, she was accepted at Harvard University with scholarship and stated that:

> "If your survival is threatened, don't just survive. Thrive."

When things look so hopeless and something bad happens to the extent that our survival itself is threatened, let's think about thriving, not just survival. Thinking about Khadijah who overcame such dire circumstances, let's have hope and courage in the face of the difficulties that we are facing at this moment. And, as to how we would be able to do that, the main message of this book is to highlight that our worldly efforts to do it our own are inherently limited, and maintaining such positive viewpoint and attitude is possible only when we fully trust the Almighty God who has the steadfast love and purpose for each of us.

In my dad's case, he was born into a relatively wealthy household, and he was a young man with so much potential for a bright future. All of this changed as he began to pursue his dream to be a lawyer, he one day started to have problems with his eyesight due to some unknown causes and malnutrition. He went into his studies without his parents' financial support mainly because my grandfather was against him continuing with his study as he wanted him to stay and take over the family business of running the farm and managing the property. When I read his book, I learned how desperate he was when he became blind at such a young and vibrant age and he stated that his hairs turned completely white due to the extreme stress on his body and mind and he lost so much weight and the will to go on. He was depressed to the level of having suicidal thoughts, but in such a mysterious manner, he was called by God when he heard a voice asking, "Why are you here? Go home and go to church!" when he was resting at a remote Buddhist temple as arranged by his parents. When he heard that voice, there was no one around, and he could not resist such a strong spirit's compelling, so he left the temple that evening and went home. Since then, he turned his ways from being a strict atheist to the devout believer.

To my father, sudden blindness was indeed a wholly life-threatening crisis that could have destroyed his life at that time. I know how difficult it is to live a life without eyesight as I have witnessed it during my childhood. Daily small tasks to big things are equally challenging and difficult for a blind person. However, I am so grateful that he chose to live, instead of ending his life, chose to commit his life to God, rather than giving up and chose to be positive more so than other people with such an amazing sense of humor and affirmative mindset, instead of staying pessimistic when he was confronted with a truly life-threatening crisis. I firmly believe that his life is a living example of thriving by the grace of

God when we voluntarily and willfully choose God as our Lord and Savior in the face of adversity. And because of his life, I can't just simply complain and despair when terrible things happen, or things don't work out the way I planned, because he has overcome such insurmountable challenges in his life, and I have witnessed that when we trust Him, all things are indeed possible no matter how difficult it may be.

# 4. Pain

## (1) Oprah's Interview

Oprah Winfrey once interviewed four female prisoners who were detained for having killed their own infant babies impulsively and out of frustration when they were physically tired, stressed, exhausted or under the influence of alcohol/drugs as the babies continued crying, refused to eat, spat out the food they tried to feed or threw tantrums. One of them threw her baby against the wall so hard causing instant death, while the others put the crying baby in the freezer or beat to death. Oprah said she tried her best not to have preconceived judgments about these women because as an interviewer, she needed to maintain a professional and neutral attitude without judgment or prejudice; however, she could not avoid feeling that these are horrible people who killed innocent young ones. As the interview progressed Oprah shed uncontrollable tears hearing these four women's tragic stories of repentance and regret about their unforgivable sin, all expressing a deep sense of remorse and self-hatred for having committed such hideous crimes.

However, Oprah said that she was extremely shocked by one particular realization about these women. Initially, she started the interview not being able to shake off the condemnation and judgment about these women for she had no idea how they could commit such horrible crimes, but as the interview went on, she somehow could see these were just ordinary women who had sufferings and problems like all of us, but they just happened to make such fatal mistake at that particular moment and they were just paying the price by being imprisoned. She could not sense that they were particularly monstrous or evil as they were all so ordinary people who had huge regret on that day they made such inconceivable mistake and each of them were living a life of pain and regret. Oprah shared that one of the interviewees said after the interview, "I can't believe you don't hate us." And to that Oprah responded, "No, I don't hate you because I see that's what you did with your pain. And I do something else with mine."

Perhaps there may be some people who have not experienced any hardship in life in achieving something valuable, but most people do have a measure of pain, hardship, challenges and sometimes unbearable suffering and achieve something despite all that or especially because of that. The difference may be in the slightest instant that they chose to endure rather than erupt, stay silent rather than vent out, and encourage oneself rather than give up at one specific moment. The decision to give up or not could take a split second and the difference in mind may be only one degree different from the previously held negative views that makes the balance tip toward positive to 51:49 from 50:50, but such tiny moments are accumulated over time and can result in the formidable force of change towards a miraculous deliverance and achievement.

"Hardships often prepare ordinary people for an extraordinary destiny."

– C.S. Lewis

Oprah Winfrey was born in January 1954 and she is known as the "Queen of All Media", having mastered her career as a prominent talk show host, movie producer, actress and entrepreneur who owns, among others, the Oprah Winfrey Network and Harpo

Productions. Furthermore, she does so much charity work for various meaningful causes. According to Wikipedia[5], she currently lives on "The Promised Land", the 42-acre estate with ocean and mountain views in Montecito, California and, as of 2014, she has a net worth in excess of $2.9 billion. However, we are well aware of all the challenges and hardships she experienced while growing up.

> "Winfrey was born into poverty in rural Mississippi to a teenage single mother and later raised in an inner-city Milwaukee neighborhood. She has stated that she was molested during her childhood and early teens and became pregnant at 14; her son died in infancy… Her mother, Vernita Lee was a housemaid…After Winfrey's birth, her mother traveled north and Winfrey spent her first six years living in rural poverty with her maternal grandmother, Hattie Mae (Presley) Lee (April 15, 1900 - February 27, 1963), who was so poor that Winfrey often wore dresses made of potato sacks, for which the local children made fun of her. Her grandmother taught her to read before the age of three and took her to the local church, where she was nicknamed "The Preacher" for her ability to recite Bible verses. When Winfrey was a child, her grandmother would hit her with a stick when she did not do chores or if she misbehaved

---

5) https://en.wikipedia.org/wiki/Oprah_Winfrey

in any way… Winfrey has stated she was molested by her cousin, uncle, and a family friend, starting when she was nine years old, something she first announced to her viewers on a 1986 episode of her TV show regarding sexual abuse." (Wikipedia[6])

Let's take a hypothetical vote about a woman who was born to a teenage single mother and was sexually abused from eight or nine years old and then became pregnant at the age of 14, and ask ten people about their views on the life prospect of this woman. I imagine that nine or ten would vote that this woman would most likely turn out to be a failure and her life would be a disaster. Now, let's tell them that this woman was called "arguably the world's most powerful woman" by CNN and Time.com and in 2007 USA Today ranked her as the most influential woman and most influential black person of the previous quarter-century, according to the source quoted above, and imagine their shock. In essence, Oprah's overcoming of seemingly insurmountable obstacles and circumstances in life upholds my argument that the crisis and challenges in life are indeed neutral in terms of directing our lives toward upward or downward spiral, particularly because negative incident can't still stop a person from overcoming it and coming

---

6) https://en.wikipedia.org/wiki/Oprah_Winfrey

out stronger, wiser and more driven, and that the most powerful source of such power of heart is the belief in God and His plan for each of our lives. Oprah was no exception to having such firm belief in the Savior.

> "I have a church with myself: I have church walking down the street. I believe in God force that lives inside all of us, and once you tap into that, you can do anything"
>
> – Oprah Winfrey

In my view, her interviews are more genuine, heart-warming and powerful than any other talk show hosts in the world, and that's why she could inspire and influence so many people out there, helping them to overcome their undesirable thoughts and habits, and move towards a better future that God has in mind for all of us.

## (2) Perfect Storm

What kinds of struggles or challenges are we faced with at this moment? We may feel fortunate for having lived a relatively peaceful life or perhaps we have gone through unbelievably tough times so far. The term, "Perfect Storm" was popularized by Sebastian Junger as follows:

> "A "perfect storm" is an expression that describes an event where a rare combination of circumstances will aggravate a situation drastically. The term is also used to describe an actual phenomenon that happens to occur in such a confluence, resulting in an event of unusual magnitude…Junger published his book "The Perfect Storm" in 1997 and its success brought the phrase into popular culture. Its adoption was accelerated with the release of the 2000 feature film adaptation of Junger's book. Since the release of the movie, the phrase has grown to mean any event where a situation is aggravated drastically by an exceptionally rare combination of circumstances." (Wikipedia[7])

When the perfect storm-like crisis happens in our life, we are indeed surrounded by both internal and external, undefeatable difficulties and our mere survival would be threatened. I sincerely pray that we don't go through such life-threatening perfect storms in our lives, and we should all be thankful for the ordinary life that we may be living if that is the case. However, at times we all

---

7) https://en.wikipedia.org/wiki/Perfect_storm

know that things happen, and we should be prepared for the worst possible perfect storm of our lives…

## (3) Boredom

The danger and pitfall of our lives that is completely opposite to the so-called perfect storm is the unbeatable boredom of daily routine. All of us, whether we live in a palace or a hut, a New York high-rise or log cabin in the mountain, we all live through a very similar life routine of waking up in the morning, having breakfast, going to work or do something, meeting and interacting with people, and come home to rest at night.

The repetitive routine may sometimes pose a threat on our lives in that we feel demoralized, uninterested or unhappy to the level of always complaining, being dragged to mundane life without any meaning and falling into a faulty thinking that other people's lives are far more exciting than ours; hence, ours are inferior to theirs. Or the worst-case scenario is we end up getting addicted to temporary pleasures and escapes, end up falling into temptations and make irreparable missteps, all simply because we were just so bored.

We all have more commonality than differences as human being, and the essential characteristic we share is that, "We want to live well." One day, I saw an interview of Mike Tyson, who answered somewhat defensively that "I just want to live well" to the question of the talk show host who asked why he has lived such volatile lifestyle. As a former professional boxer, even though he won a heavyweight title at the age of 20 and earned millions of dollars, he was convicted of rape and went to prison, accused of domestic violence, spousal abuse, adultery and declared bankruptcy and heavily indebted at some point, and his nickname is the "Baddest Man on the Planet", according to Wikipedia[8]. Ultimately, it is illuminating to know that everybody, even a person with extreme life style, wants to live well, but because he doesn't know 'how' to live well, he has lived his life, enslaved by his violent tendency, bad habits and addictions, sinful nature and instinctive desires and greed, rather than being led by a better source that can truly help him to live well.

---

8) https://en.wikipedia.org/wiki/Mike_Tyson

## (4) It's Up to You What You Do with Your Pain

Everybody in this world has pain. There are many challenges in this world that are common to all of us, and the rich may be frustrated with the economic structure that impose tax on their wealth and the poor may suffer from the dire conditions of their lives and even the young and healthy eventually gets old and sick. So, what's critical in our lives is what we do with our pain and how we can manage our lives in a good direction despite the pain.

My husband, Thomas shared his observation one day that I seemed to have somewhat different approach from my sister in relation to my dad, and that probably helped cultivating my communication skills and problem-solving ability. In essence, he noticed that I talk to my dad a lot more to overcome his limitations as a blind person for being unable to read my facial expression or body language; hence, unable to know what I am going through in advance unless I explain to him whereas my sister is not that talkative to that level vis-à-vis my dad. I thought about what it was like growing up and I agreed that's indeed what happened. Since young, regarding the problem of difficulty in communication with my dad, I unconsciously reacted by verbally expressing more to supplement such weakness, whereas my sister didn't, maybe because she didn't want to, or she preferred talking to other people. So, I have a more deeper relationship with my dad in terms of sharing my life experiences and problems whereas my sister is more independent in some way.

Our approach in relation to the problem was quite different and for me, I believe that my approach helped me facilitate some essential communication and creative problem-solving skills. For example, as legal service is also one of the service industries, it is critical to appreciate what the client needs and what needs to be done to solve any given problem, and back in 2009 when I was working on a project financing transaction for an Indonesian client, our team encountered a major obstacle that might deter a timely closing of the transaction because one of the syndicate lenders insisted on one condition precedent that the client could not provide. After a few rounds of failed discussions and negotiation, it almost came to a point where the deal was collapsing due to the disagreement amongst the parties on that requirement and the project may come to a halt for want of the requisite funding at that time. The client was very upset and we as the legal counsel were quite stressed over what we could do. When I stepped in to facilitate the process, however, I was able to make a creative alternative suggestion to the client's in-house legal counsel which would satisfy that lender's internal requirement for credit approval, after having spoken with the lender's representative and the client on separate occasions and appreciating what the lender needs and what the client can provide in lieu thereof. The transaction closed successfully, and the parties were very thankful for our service and facilitation. It is one of the positive experiences in my legal career that I felt quite proud that I could help through my communication and problem-solving skills. And I sometimes think about how it was cultivated in part thanks to my upbringing and my reaction to a seemingly challenging circumstance.

We all have pain and there are some people who carry an unbelievably heavy load while most of us live a relatively ordinary life with a certain degree of bearable problems and burdens. Such pain could be physical handicap, unexpected accident, mental and emotional struggles, relationship problems, deeply-held secrets and hurts that cannot be shared with anybody else, loneliness, or self-hatred for the regret over what we have done in the past and other types of burdens in our lives. Amid our pain, let us think again on what direction we are leading ourselves by making big and small decisions and make a more thoughtful choice for positive direction. It is of course quite challenging to stay optimistic in the face of devastating difficulties but if we can hold on to the unswerving faith and conviction in Almighty God who sustains our life and destiny, I am absolutely confident that we can stop ourselves from being overwhelmed by the many obstacles, peoples' criticism and our own self-blame, spinning thoughts, concerns, worries and anxiety, fear and doubts. And only when we can hold on to our faith amid such confusion and deep desolation, I am certain that we can ultimately have a beautiful and meaningful end of our pain that we never could have imagined before.

# 5.

# True Resilience

"When bad things happen, your life is not over. It's just altered."

— Maria Shriver

## (1) Life = Both Necessary and Sufficient Conditions for Resilience

The common dictionary definition of the term, "resilience" is the capacity to recover quickly from difficulties. It was merely one of the words that I had to memorize in high school, but now it has become one of the main streams of positive psychologies in that it is used as a conceptual tool to analyze each person's ability to cope with problem or difficulty. It refers to the tenacity and elasticity of mind that enables a person to bounce back from the setback and come out even stronger and better after going through a challenge. A simply analogy for resilience is comparing what happens when you drop a rubber ball vs a glass ball on the ground. One will shatter while the other bounces back. However, in my view, even the glass balls have resilience in a sense that its small pieces can be used for producing a beautiful glass art. For that proposition, I want to emphasize three points regarding the resilience that I see.

First, as long as we are alive, we all have resilience, and in that sense, life is the necessary and sufficient conditions for resilience.

The Fact that You are Alive and Living = Resilience

I am always encouraged when I see our body recovers from wounds even when we don't even apply ointment or treatment. As long as we are alive and breathing, we have the inherent ability to get better and be restored. No matter how long it takes and how slow it is, it will be healed, and we have that undeniable capacity within us.

We close our eyes and go to bed at night, but we open our eyes again in the morning because we are alive. Death means that once we close our eyes, they stay closed forever because there is no resilience to awake from eternal sleep of our being. I cried over

Sarah's death because she lied down there with her eyes closed and she would never wake up from that because there is no resilience and no life… So, with a broken heart and tears in my eyes, I dare to make the broad proposition that as long as we are alive, we have the resilience needed to overcome any difficulty or obstacle in our lives.

Second, the difference in exercising that resilience lies in whether we know 'how' to use it or not. Even if we have that capacity, if nobody tells us how to use it for maximum benefit, we won't be able to use it in any meaningful way. There are lots of new inventions and technological development on a daily basis, but even the most sophisticated machine or equipment would not make a single difference if we don't know how it works and if we never read the manual provided by the inventor. What's most critical in our lives is to know the potential, the capacity that is 'within us', and perhaps that's why Socrates stated, "Know thyself". A brief internet search seems to suggest that this statement was inscribed in the Temple of Apollo at Delphi, and not originally said by Socrates himself, but at any rate, the meaning was studied by many scholars and it is interpreted to suggest the mandate that we should strive to know ourselves and, moreover, others so that we can live our lives well in harmony.

Knowing oneself is not that easy. Knowing me truly means knowing my potential and resilience and it's an inherently challenging process in and of itself in that through the endeavors to know myself, such realization and awareness will ultimately enable more honorable objective of my life to step out and encourage and help others based on the higher understanding of and compassion towards humanity. And one of the most crucial factors in the endeavor to know myself is to acknowledge that I didn't make myself, and it is God who made me; hence, we need to learn about the manual God had in mind when creating myself. It is only when we are fully aware of and in agreement with the creator's manual, then we can draw maximum benefit from ourselves and live our lives to the fullest. In other words, we need the humility to acknowledge that we cannot succeed in knowing us, because we didn't make ourselves, and the effort to know ourselves is incomplete without knowing the loving perspective of God for us and our lives. Let us always strive to know and fully appreciate His love, grace and forgiveness and live our lives in accordance with His grand plan for each of our lives.

Third, resilience is not limited to bouncing back to an original status, but rather it is a possibility for change and ultimate transformation into something else. When a glass or mirror is broken into pieces, it is easy to conclude that there is no resilience and it's just wasted. However, from a thoughtful artist's perspective, each broken piece can still be valuable resource to complete a beautiful art piece.

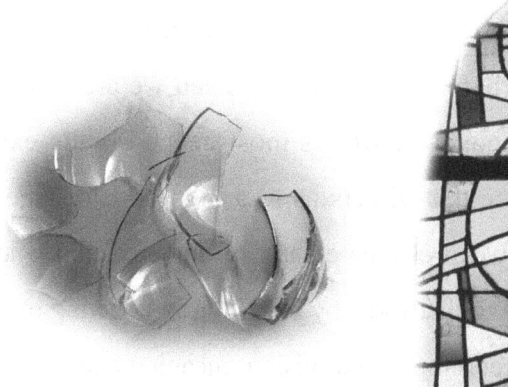

When something bad happens in our lives, we may lament on the implication that we can't go back to the previous condition, but what we need to do is to focus on the possibility that we can become something else and live a much more meaningful life than before despite that unfortunate incident or happening. Resilience is an upward spiral for or toward something better or more meaningful, rather than a neutral trait or character in and of itself. It is a potent energy that can move all of us toward a positive direction, rather than a stagnant trait that inherently exists in only certain people. As long as we are alive, we have that flexibility and capacity to change for the better towards an upward spiral. In other words, the seemingly unbearable difficulty in our lives is an opportunity to transform ourselves and have a new life different than before. And perhaps, with that new opportunity, our lives can have much more significance and influence on others, which was not possible before the incident. When we are completely hopeless and despondent, what's most needed is the external force and guidance that directs us to a higher vision, meaning and hope that derives from the creator of universe, and when we react affirmatively to that force by believing in it, acting on it and living our lives according to that vision, meaning and hope, there is no limit to what can be achieved through that resilience and transformation.

## (2) Soul Surfer

Soul Surfer is a movie released in 2011 and a biographical film based on the real-life experiences of Bethany Hamilton who started surfing as little as three years old but then lost one arm from a horrible shark attack during a surfing practice when she was only 13 years old. The accident was life-threatening because she lost almost 60% of her blood due to the loss of her left arm and the doctor who treated her immediately after the accident doesn't hesitate to define her recovery and survival a miracle. During the surgery, recovery and the process to get used to the lifestyle with one arm only and eventual return to the ocean to continue with her life as a professional surfer, she maintained such strong faith and conviction in Jesus Christ and stayed positive despite the unbearable pain and difficulty for having to re-learn to surf with the unexpected handicap. Since the accident, she not only continued to live the life of a surfer that she wanted since little, but also lived the inspiring life to support and help others to learn about God and His love toward us.

She set up the charitable foundation called 'Friends of Bethany' and travel around to encourage other amputees like herself and lead people into the life of faith. At the core of her resilience and capacity to recover and transform into more influential role than a mere sports woman is the relentless faith that even dedicated her life to Jesus Christ at the age of five. She said that she was so encouraged by the promise of God set out in Jeremiah when she was so saddened and lost hope for the future due to the unexpected incident.

> "For I know the plans I have for you," declares the Lord, "plans to prosper you and not to harm you, plans to give you hope and a future." (Jeremiah 29:11)

At the end of the movie, when the interviewer asks whether she would take if there is a chance to undo the loss of her arm, she responds that she would still lose it because she can embrace more people now without one arm than she could ever with both arms. Her sense of mission and purpose in life through the life-threatening tragedy shed light on the darkness in this world in that even in the worst possible scenario, God can still revive and sustain the hope in all of us and lead us into a path that is so much more meaningful and influential that before.

## (3) Flexibility to Know that There is No One Single Right Answer to My Life

When we are faced with the unexpected challenge or suffer from external or internal threat to question the validity of our lives, it is so easy to deteriorate into the downward spiral because we are submerged by an erroneous conviction that there is no point even trying or a mixture of whole negative sentiments such as confusion, doubt, hopelessness and despair. We can't help but focusing on the fact that the incident left an indelible mark on our lives, and it can never recover, and the only thing left to do is to just give up and end it. But as we have seen in the cases of Oprah and Bethany, the unforeseen accident and unfortunate upbringing could present a precious opportunity for us to expand our horizons and move toward more positive and meaningful direction.

I cautiously argue that Oprah may not have such exceptional success as a talk show host if she did not have such horrific life experiences earlier in her life as she would not be so deeply sympathetic towards so many millions of people out there. Likewise, Bethany would not be able to inspire and encourage numerous people and ultimately become the heroine in the movie that is made in celebration of her being such a remarkable role model of faith but for the unbearably painful accident at such an early stage of her life.

Looking around, my brother wanted to live an ordinary life of a salary employee as he majored in computer engineering at university, but he had the unfortunate incident during the mandatory military service in Korea where he injured his back and due to the failed surgery, he now has a life-long handicap of nerve and muscle problem in his back that frequently causes excruciating pain through his back and legs. While recovering from the botched disc surgery, he agonized over the predicament and pain and at some point, ultimately responded to God's calling that he should commit his life to His service although he has rejected the prayers and wishes of our dad to become a pastor in the past, for he knew how hard it is to live the life of a pastor and he wanted to avoid that calling and just live a life of ordinary Christian, rather than becoming a pastor.

Same with my dad in that while he was at the verge of ending his life out of desperation when he became blind, he was drastically saved by God to be a Christian and eventually called to be a pastor through that turning point in his life. That's why I think it is so important to have the flexibility and open-mindedness to believe that there is no one single right answer to my life, but rather there are so many possibilities, and anything is indeed possible if we remain in faith. However, this kind of assertion should be made in such a careful manner because none of us are in a position to even appreciate how deep the pain and agony was if we were in that person's shoes when faced with such life-threatening crisis. While it is true that both my dad and my brother diligently fulfill the vision that God has provided and endeavor to completely rejoice everyday in obedience to God's command to do so, living a life as a handicapped person with physical challenge and ongoing piercing pain is not easy by any stretch of the imagination.

Like Oprah, Bethany, my brother and my dad, all of us live our respective lives faced with unique problems, heartache and loss that nobody else can truly appreciate. It could be visible or physical challenges, hidden dark scars, secrets, deficiencies or predicaments like loneliness, sadness and depression that we must live with for the rest of our lives. But having seen the incredible potential as in the cases of Oprah and Bethany, let us not easily conclude that there is no hope and resort to self-destructive solutions to the problems; rather, take the courage of heart to step out in the path of our lives towards a wiser, stronger and meaningful purpose.

### (4) Be Thankful

Oprah once said that whenever she is faced with a bewildering crisis, the first thing she does no matter what is to 'be thankful' because no matter how bad it is, she knows that her faith is so strong that she will overcome, and she will come out stronger and wiser, enjoying the beauty of life more so than before because of that difficulty. Also, she said that amid despair, she thinks about her heart that continues to beat despite her hopelessness, her other body parts that are diligently fulfilling their roles to sustain her livelihood and be filled with gratitude. I think we should all appreciate our body whenever we want to give up because we are hurt, saddened or upset and with that gratitude, we will be able to restore the courage of heart to stand up and carry on with our lives with the unbelievable tenacity to go on toward a positive direction no matter how upsetting and disappointing the current conditions may be.

# 6.
# My Mistakes Don't Define Me

"Our sins don't define the whole picture of who we are."
— Ted Kennedy

## (1) The Bitter Roots of Shame, Guilt and Fear

Some of the leading and most common negative feelings that we experience through our lives would be shame, guilt and fear. It would be perfect if we can live, never making any mistakes and never encountering any unforeseen challenges, but there can be many accidents and unfortunate problems that happen to us that may result in fear, resentment and anxiety, as well as internal self-doubt, guilt and shame for the repetitive blunders we make through our lives. Those unhelpful emotions prevent us from living the life to its fullest as the children of God making positive and meaningful choices every day toward the fulfilment of God's vision of loving ourselves and our neighbors. That is why we need the help of a powerful force from the above as I have seen in Singapore, and the core message of this book is to emphasize that it is only the Gospel of God's everlasting love and salvation that could solve seemingly impossible problems of our lives, help us overcome the strong temptations of devil to deceive us by using the traps of negative feelings while preventing us from seeing the potential in us, teach and show us the plans that He has for each of us, and ultimately enable us to live our lives to the best way possible.

> "For the Spirit God gave us does not make us timid, but gives us power, love and self-discipline." (2 Timothy 1:7)

The bible says that all negative feelings like guilt, shame and fear are from devil, not from God. The devil uses these negative emotions as snares to subjugate ourselves under their influence and control for us to continue to complain and stay skeptical, pessimistic and hopeless, to be susceptible to give up and mistrust ourselves and other people, to make undesirable and damaging choices in life and to commit the eventual self-destructive act of ending our lives with our own hands. In stark contrast, God accepts us as we are unconditionally, loves us as His own children, saves us from our condemned destiny for eternal deliverance, expects us to live each day full of joy and hope for the future, and inspires and guides us to be able to love ourselves and our neighbors as our own in resemblance of Him, living a life of light that shines in the world that is full of darkness.

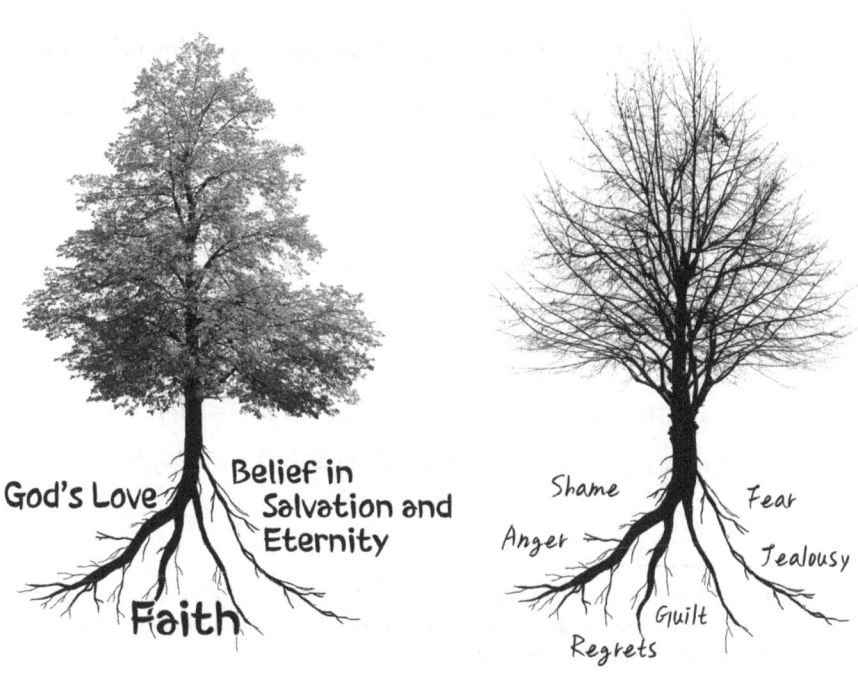

The expression of this chapter, "My mistakes don't define me." is a simple adaptation of the statement made by Senator Edward Moore "Ted" Kennedy who stated as follows in an interview regarding his book, entitled "True Compass"[9]:

> "…Do I think it tells the whole story of character? No, I truly do not. Men and women are more complicated than that. Some people make mistakes and try to learn from them and do better. Our sins don't define the whole picture of who we are."

Ted Kennedy has lived a truly dramatic and yet so inspiring and majestic life, and the following is an excerpt of the relevant parts from Wikipedia[10]:

> "Edward Moore "Ted" Kennedy (February 22, 1932 - August 25, 2009) was an American politician who served as a United States Senator from Massachusetts for over forty years from 1962 until his death in 2009. He was the youngest of the nine children of Joseph P. Kennedy Sr.

---

9) http://www.dailymail.co.uk/news/article-1210930/Ted-Kennedy-memoir-reveals-guilt-inexcusable--terrible-decisions-Chappaquiddick-woman-Mary-Jo-Kopechnes-death.html
10) https://en.wikipedia.org/wiki/Ted_Kennedy

and Rose Fitzgerald···He attended ten different schools by the age of eleven, with his education suffering as a result. Between the ages of eight and sixteen, Ted suffered the traumas of Rosemary's failed lobotomy and the deaths of Joseph Jr. in war and Kathleen in an airplane crash··· Ted attended Harvard College. At the end of his second semester in May 1951, Kennedy was anxious about maintaining his eligibility for athletics for the next year, and he had a classmate take his place at a Spanish language examination. The ruse was immediately discovered and both students were expelled for cheating··· A member of the Democratic Party, he was the second most senior member of the Senate when he died and is the fourth-longest-continuously-serving senator in United States history, having served there for almost 47 years···Ted Kennedy was 30 years old when he first entered the Senate in 1962··· On June 19, 1964, Kennedy was a passenger in a private Aero Commander 680 airplane that was flying in bad weather from Washington to Massachusetts. The plane crashed into an apple orchard···and Kennedy was pulled from the wreckage and spent months in a hospital recovering from a severe back injury, a punctured lung, broken ribs and internal bleeding. He suffered chronic back pain for the rest of his life as a result of the accident··· The Chappaquiddick incident in 1969 resulted in the death of his automobile passenger, Mary Jo Kopechne. Kennedy pleaded guilty to a charge of leaving the scene of an accident and later received a two-month suspended sentence. The incident and its aftermath hindered his chances of ever becoming President… He became recognized as "The Lion of the Senate" through his long tenure and influence. Kennedy and his staff wrote more than 300 bills that were enacted into law. Unabashedly liberal, Kennedy championed an interventionist government that emphasized economic and social justice, but he was also known for working with Republicans to find compromises among senators with disparate views."

In a sense, Ted had tumultuous upbringing, made some serious mistakes, and went through vastly hurtful experiences including the assassination of his two brothers John F. Kennedy and Robert F. Kennedy, let alone the death of two siblings when he was little, but nonetheless, he never gave up and continued to commit his life to the mission of achieving social and economic justice as a lawyer and senator, ultimately being called as "The Lion of the Senate". His life course and his statement above inspire me to see myself and others in a more positive and generous light despite many shortcomings and imperfections. Our faults are not the determining factor that defines our respective identities. What's most important is whether we deeply regret and repent our mistake, learn from it, and resolve to not repeat the same and work very hard and do better.

I will share some of my regrets and flaws in my life for purposes of encouraging readers to not give up no matter what. I tend to repeat the same mistake, which makes me feel so shameful and regretful, and combined with the sense of guilt and condemnation, such negative emotions often torture my mind. For example, I frequently changed jobs after I became a lawyer. While I was receiving positive feedback from the firms that I was working at, I decided to move to a new one in most cases when I received an offer. The first law firm that I worked after articling in Canada was by far the largest that I worked for, and it was such an amazing place that specialized in project finance and there were many seasoned partners who were role models in many respects. While attending intensive training programs held in London and Hong Kong, I undertook various projects, drafting various contracts and interacting and negotiating with clients, counterparts and their counsels. I learned a lot and there were so many good things the firm offered, and the partners were supportive. However, I couldn't get along with a colleague, who was extremely ambitious and for whatever reason, I just felt somewhat fearful around her perhaps because of her overly-manipulative and competitive attitude, having heard of her tragic and abusive happenings in her family when growing up in the poor region of India. So, I decided to move to another law firm in less than two years.

Looking back, it was such an unwise misstep that I gave up on the good opportunity just because I was uncomfortable around somebody and in this regard, I want to advise any fresh-graduates who start a new career that we should hold on to the first job at least three years no matter what. There may be temptations to move and hope it would be better in the next place, but the best thing to do is to stay on and learn as much as possible in the first opportunity that comes to us. Second advice that I want to give is to not be influenced by other people's words. At the time of my departure, five or six lawyers were leaving around the same time, and one of them went around telling people that the firm was a 'sinking ship', and we should all move out. I was shamefully influenced by such remarks and felt compelled that I should leave as soon as possible. In a sense, I focused on the negative while there were so many positives at the first law firm that I worked for.

My next firm scouted me with a better offer and I continued to focus on international financial transactions under the leadership of a female partner, who happened to be a mother of two kids and such a distinguished role model as a working mother in many respects. As a Malaysian lady, she is now the head of that British law firm's Singapore office. However, at that time there were three senior associates within our team, who were close friends with each other and two of them are now a married couple and at one point, I unfortunately had a small conflict with one of them and since then it somehow became a bit difficult to work with them and I started to think that perhaps I should have a fresh start elsewhere. The third law firm approached me aggressively that one of the partners said she was so impressed by my professionalism when she was working on the other side of the transaction once and she really wanted to work with me. So, I again moved to her firm and yet soon after I learned that this firm was quite unique in that it had one primary client based in Indonesia that took up almost 90% of our work in corporate and finance practice group. While I did not intend to become an Indonesia expert, all my work, negotiation, dealings with people, counterparts and law firms were related to Indonesia and I had to travel to Indonesia on various occasions. So, I thought about my career development as to which way to go, and then ultimately decided to go back to Korea wrapping up my overseas' life experiences after 12 years.

When I interviewed with Yulchon at the end of 2010, the partners asked several times why I moved so often, and while I was fully aware of how difficult decision it was each time as there were definitely pros and cons that I agonized over whether to stay or move on, I realized that such frequent moves just don't look good on a resume. Also in Singapore changing jobs was viewed more favorably as sign of someone in high demand at that time and I was influenced by such views, but the bottom line is that companies value commitment, and I totally understand the prospective employer's concern in that regard. Since then, I am very proud that I worked at Yulchon close to seven years and it is all thanks to the strong leadership and excellent work environment.

When I look back on these mistakes in my career, I feel a lot of regret and at times it feels like there is no hope in my career development since I screwed up by changing so often at the very beginning. However, I also encourage myself that the choice is in front of me either to be confined by negative feelings like shame, regret and fear of not being able to have a fruitful career or to nonetheless have hope and faith that I can still try to do my best and continue to rebuild my career despite the challenges. In fact, I learned a lot through changing jobs a few times because I could see how different firms operate getting exposed to different approaches to work and meetings and interacting with many different people from all walks of lives. I believe that I have broader perspective and flexible and open mindset because I was exposed to three different law firms during the five-year period I worked at UK law firms in Singapore. Therefore, let us not just live with a defeatist attitude when we make mistakes, but ensure that we truly repent and try to look at the positive and resolve to do better next time and move on towards a positive direction.

While it was embarrassing for me to provide this detailed account of my career missteps as a professional, I did so with the purpose of helping others to learn from my mistakes and raise awareness that even if we change jobs with the best of intentions, there may be totally unpredicted challenges in the next place and we should all take that into account before we make a premature decision to give up and move on. It was always like that for me in that there was always something that made me feel uncomfortable or unprepared for whenever I moved and what was most critical in each circumstance was how I maintained my positive perspective and attitude, rather than expecting that people and things are exactly as I hoped for or most ideal from my vantage point. No matter what unexpected obstacles life presents, let us maintain our optimistic mindset, making conscientiously constructive choices so that our lives are moving towards the direction of an upward spiral.

In addition to the negative feelings of regret and shame when we make repetitive mistakes, the ancillary feelings of guilt tend to follow because it is quite logical to blame ourselves when we make such errors, and in my case, the sense of guilt was and is quite dominant in that I wasted God's blessing in being granted with such amazing opportunities to work in excellent UK law firms and I, instead of staying positive, continued to complain, looked at negatives only, and gave up easily. Furthermore, there is a stronger sense of guilt for having lived a selfish lifestyle just focusing on career success and personal achievement, rather than spending time and efforts to help others who are in need. We are supposed to encourage each other, helping those in need such as the weak, the young, the handicapped and the vulnerable. In particular, the fact that I could not even help my own sister has given me an enormous sense of guilt for my selfish lifestyle focusing on my own wellbeing and happiness only. But I take that painful reflection as an opportunity to change myself and redirect my life to a more meaningful and positive direction, rather than getting overwhelmed by the disapproving sentiments of shame and guilt and sincerely hope that I could encourage other people who may suffer from similar regrets.

Another harmful feeling that could have a major impact on our lives is fear. Let me share one experience that had a lasting impact on my life that cultivated an unconscious fear of poverty and decision-making. When my dad became blind, he became a professional acupuncturist and successful such that many celebrities and athletes came for treatment at that time. And we were relatively well off, living in a big house with a beautiful garden, with a couple of live-in helpers and a chauffeur-driven car during the late 1970s and early 80s.

However, my father suddenly declared to us one day that he decided to start a full-time ministry and he sold the house we were living in at that time and bought a church in Byondong, located in the western part of Daejeon when I was a fourth grader in elementary school in 1984. He said that we needed to move to a corner room of that house so that the new owner could move in until the church was ready for our move. So, six of our family members, my parents, me and my three siblings, together with our maternal grandmother who lived with us at that time all squeezed into one small room divided by bookshelves to create some boundaries between my parents and the rest. I remember peeping my dad handing over an envelope to the driver, wishing him well and the car was one day gone as he sold it off.

It was such a shock to me when we were forced into that kind of drastic change in my early teen year and I think it somehow left an indelible impression on my mind that you can suddenly be so poor in an instant. Even when we moved into the place attached to the church that my dad had purchased, I was deeply dismayed to see the small and dark space without any resemblance to the previous house we lived in. Since then, I regrettably acted out at times and expressed my frustration and resentment towards my parents for putting me in that kind of misery and had a somewhat troubled adolescence growing up.

What's surprising to me sometimes though is that I suffer from the fear of poverty and decision-making probably because of that incident growing up, and I must consciously resolve to be free from those fears, get rid of their bitter roots and move on to live my life to the full achievement of the grand vision of God's plan for my life and sharing His love with other people.

In sum, all these negative emotions of regret, guilt, shame and fear are just a few examples of instruments that the devil uses to enthrall us to live a restrained life rather than to the full as promised by God. Nobody is entirely free from the influence of negative sentiments at least once in our lives and it is impossible to live a life feeling 100% perfect all the time. And such negative feelings and condemnation function like bitter roots that destroy the viability of the tree itself and threatening our wellbeing. Our life choices stemming from bitter roots would not be able to help us grow strongly so that we can be of benefit to people around us sharing our shade and many fruits. Therefore, it is so important that we deal with the negative feelings cautiously and effectively and ultimately get rid of the bitter roots and replace them with the good roots of faith and conviction based on God's love.

## (2) My Dreams, Hope and Calling Define Me

If our mistakes, regrets, and sins do not define us, what define us then? What determines our identities? In my view, the specific dream, hope, calling and vision that we have inevitably because of where we are situated at this moment is the fundamental aspect of what defines each of us. Isn't it so exciting and heart-warming to think about the limitless potential that the positive thinking and the hope for the better future define us? And, I truly believe that that positive thinking is most powerful and meaningful when it is based on the firm conviction in the specific plan that God has for each of us. Ted Kennedy said as follows when he gave a concession speech back in 1980 Democratic National Convention running against Jimmy Carter for the Democratic presidential nomination:

> "For me, a few hours ago, this campaign came to an end. For all those whose cares have been our concern, the work goes on, the cause endures, the hope still lives, and the dream shall never die."

The endeavor to overcome the deep-rooted pain in our hearts, regrets and shame, unavoidable guilt and fear is a life-long process, and it will probably go on until the moment we die. However,

I wish all of us can have the courage of heart to go on and let hope live and dream never die as Kennedy has done to fulfill his mission as senator to enact laws to enhance socio-economic justice despite the baggage of physical pain, mental and emotional scars for having made so many mistakes in life and for being subject to such unbelievable tragedies of having the siblings assassinated for no reason and being the target of peoples' negative criticisms and bad reputation. At the funeral of his assassinated brother, Robert Kennedy, Ted delivered the following eulogy[11]:

> "My brother need not be idealized, or enlarged in death beyond what he was in life; to be remembered simply as a good and decent man, who saw wrong and tried to right it, saw suffering and tried to heal it, saw war and tried to stop it. Those of us who loved him and who take him to his rest today, pray that what he was to us and what he wished for others will someday come to pass for all the world. As he said many times, in many parts of this nation, to those he touched and who sought to touch him: "Some men see things as they are and say why. I dream things that never were and say why not.""

---

11) https://en.wikipedia.org/wiki/Ted_Kennedy

The question raised by a person who believes in God's vision and exerting his or her best despite the unbearable challenges and obstacles asking, 'why not' will embarrass the cynic's complaint and obvious question of 'why me', focusing on the unfortunate incident and negative environment. The shift in our perspective from the negative to the positive is possible only through the wholesome faith in God's love and plan for our lives in no matter how dark the circumstance we are in may be, and through being firmly rooted in such dreams, hopes, and mission in our lives, we will be led to the path of an exquisite upward spiral.

### (3) Knowing Me Accurately

In order to know the dreams and calling in our lives and have a steadfast hope and faith to maintain a positive attitude even amid the darkest moment of our lives, we need to know exactly who we are as Socrates stated, and "Know Thyself" is not a simple proposition in that only when you truly know and appreciate yourself, everything else stems from it and it is a complex process of deliberation, awareness, realization and enlightenment in various aspects. And once we truly get to know ourselves, we inevitably learn to live with others in harmony respecting and encouraging each other leading a virtuous cycle of an upward spiral, rather than living as an isolated island. In this regard, I want to share five essential elements that I think are important in knowing ourselves accurately.

First, each of us consists of a mind, body and spirit, and all three realms make up our existence organically influencing and interacting with each other in one way or another. In a sense, a believer is a person who invited the Holy Spirit to reside in his or her spirit, following its guidance and bearing the fruits of the Holy Spirit. However, there are unfortunately people who are possessed by the evil spirit living a life of greed, false ideas and vice, and that is the reason that we are mandated to spread the good news of Gospel to transform people. This book is my small attempt to obey such God's command to share the Gospel of His love.

> "But the fruit of the Spirit is love, joy, peace, long suffering, gentleness, goodness, faithfulness, meekness and self-control. Against such things there is no law." (Galatians 5:22-23)

The soul is where our thoughts and emotions come from and interact with each other, and the appreciation of the mind-body-soul connection is so critical to effectively deal with our life problems and weaknesses. In principle, I believe we can manage and operate in the most positive way if we are led by the Holy Spirit in the spiritual realm, rather than working on improving on our physical health and wellbeing, focusing on our emotional recovery and balance only, and that's why I keep emphasizing the importance of faith in God and awareness of His plan for each of us. While trying to feel better by working out and listening to inspiring music, for example, may work to a certain extent, there is an inherent limitation to such efforts as the spiritual sphere is ultimately more powerful in directing our lives in a certain direction, and if we are led or influenced by the evil spirit, no matter how hard we try to feel better, we just can't overcome the barrier at some point and end up in despair and misery.

Second, we have a certain tendency that we are born with or cultivated through nurture. It could be positive or negative, and that propensity impacts our identity in many ways. For instance, we could have the predisposition to prefer certain music, food and people, we tend to feel easily upset, sad or excited, and we definitely tend to react in certain way to certain stimulus in our lives. I tend to feel strong responsibility whenever I am given a specific task, and I prefer spicy food. Knowing our tendency would help us understand our identity and what's important is to enhance our virtuous inclinations and work on our negative predispositions to minimize the harmful implication.

Third, we have both merits and demerits, or plus and minus points, which are somewhat distinct from strengths and weakness which I discuss below, and there is no one who is perfect. For me, I am somewhat good at communication thanks in part to my efforts to communicate with my blind father by elaborating more since my early years, while such merit functions as a double-edged sword in that it tends to make me complain a lot too at times. My husband told me that I say, "I am so tired" so often when I don't even have to say it cause it's just so obvious from my facial expression and demeanor. I appreciate his feedback and humbly reflect on my shortcomings and resolve to overcome it. I fully acknowledge that especially after I gave birth to my second child, I continuously complain that it's just so hard. I never felt so exhausted when I was just working with no kids because I focused on the work and there were no major distractions.

However, even my mother who doesn't talk that much once told me, "Stop complaining. You have such beautiful children, and if you keep saying that it's so hard, it discourages people around you, too." I felt so sorry to my mom because I remembered how my mother was doing dishes and house chores, carrying our youngest brother on her back and never complained… The images of her sacrifice and dedication for the blind husband, his ministry and four children make me feel ashamed about my selfish attitude and complaint over the task of taking care of only two kids, especially with the caring support of my husband in many respects.

Just to make a slight diversion, I never cried over work no matter how difficult or overwhelming it was working at big law firms so far for the last decade because I truly enjoyed the responsibility and the type of work. However, within several days of having decided to be the full-time caretaker, I cried while changing the diaper of my daughter at home because I suddenly lost the strength of my heart as I compared myself with my previous self who managed and undertook so many projects, interacting with adults, rather than infants. I love my kids so much but being a stay-at-home mom is so much more difficult than working outside, and besides there is no financial reward for staying at home. I felt so dejected and furthermore felt that there is some structural problem in our society thinking about many mothers out there who may face similar doubts and fears. Working means we are just responsible for the tasks that are given to us, and we do our best as a team member whereas being a mother means we are responsible for someone else's life 100% 24/7. The essence of responsibility is so different, and the latter can be at times overwhelming with no remuneration, which is why it is called a 'labor of love'. I remember sharing a sentiment that working moms feel so peaceful when we come to the office although we love our children so much. It is a proven fact that so many stay-at-home mothers suffer from post-partum depression and many women's career potential is cut short because of the burden of childcare, and I sincerely hope that there is some structural solution to these problems. Anne-Marie Slaughter wrote a book, entitled "Unfinished Business: Women, Men, Work, Family", which is published in Korea as well, and I agree with her proposal that there should be a change in perspective that childcare is viewed as a shared responsibility for both men and women and there should be some systematic support in public policy to enable such change in our society.

Fourth, to know ourselves, we need to appreciate our strengths and weakness, and utilize our strengths and complement the weakness, which again may be genetic or cultivated through nurture, education and experience. For instance, my strength is that I am good at English as a native Korean speaker to a certain extent and my weakness is that I am not good at math. While I started to learn English from junior high school only, I can express myself relatively well in English.

On the other hand, I lost interest in math in high school maybe because I did not have a good teacher, or I just don't have a talent whatsoever in that subject. It is unfortunate that I have such weakness, but I do my best to not lose hope and supplement that weakness to the extent possible.

Lastly, knowing ourselves means that we need to honestly see ourselves as we are and understand the multiple aspects of ourselves before we make any decision or choice in our lives. When faced with negative incident, the simple fight-or-flight response is not advisable, and it would not have a positive outcome ultimately. The common dictionary definition of the fight-or-flight response (also called hyperarousal or the acute stress response) available in Wikipedia[12] is "a physiological reaction that occurs in response to a perceived harmful event, attack or threat to survival." As explained above, we need to understand that we are made of mind, body and spirit, having certain tendencies with merits and demerits as well as strengths and weaknesses, and knowing the current status and condition accurately would help us to make positive choices in whatever situation we are in. Perhaps such a cautious approach may appear somewhat artificial and awkward in comparison with the natural fight-or-flight response, but resorting to such a natural response to confront or run away to hide in isolation does not separate us from other animals.

In addition, what's critical in the process is that such a deliberate response would require some time. We need to pray to God and the Holy Spirit to guide us to make the wise choice under the given circumstances. When our feelings and thoughts are leaning towards a negative direction, we need to ponder upon the reason and the ways to improve and make necessary changes. In any situation, patience and a cautious approach is always better than the simple fight-or-flight reaction that seemed so natural at that particular moment. Furthermore, I strongly believe

---

12) https://en.wikipedia.org/wiki/Fight-or-flight_response

that understanding ourselves in this way helps us to have more generosity and compassion towards other people around us to appreciate what they are facing and struggling with. Perhaps they are not aware of their inherent tendency and need to overcome it, maybe their weakness may be complemented and become a strength, and perhaps they just don't know how to find ways to react better in a conscientious manner and end up just resorting to the simplistic and unreflected way of reaction without any deliberation and continue to make repetitive mistakes going down the path of a downward spiral. Perhaps what is most enlightening and instructive in some sense is that we should stay humble to appreciate that the task of 'knowing ourselves' is not simple at all and is indeed a life-long work in progress.

### (4) Humility to Acknowledge Mistakes and Resolution to Do Better

We all have pride to a certain degree, and a balanced pride in the form of self-esteem is necessary and beneficial. However, unbalanced and distorted pride is not desirable and harmful in many respects. In principle, if we think we are better than others, that is inherently wrong. Those who treat others based on that attitude will always have problems in a relationship. Healthy self-esteem comes from self-respect as well as respecting others around us; furthermore, ideal self-esteem based on Christianity and conscientiousness will always accompany absolute humility and a humble mindset, and not easily be offended or blame others but rather always reflect on oneself before pointing fingers at others. Even when we encounter a relationship problem, a person with a balanced self-esteem will humbly reflect and repent, resolve to not repeat the mistake and to do better going forward whereas those with a slanted pride would deny any wrongdoing and blame others, the environment, or any injustice done to them and end up growing bitter roots in mind enslaved by the prejudice, lopsided and negative thoughts. If we made mistakes, we should not be so thick-skinned that we refuse to acknowledge our fault and point fingers at others; rather, we should have the maturity and humility to accept the responsibility and move on with the firm resolution that we should do better next. Moreover, what I want to underscore in this process of reflection and resolution is also that we should not be overwhelmed by guilt and hopelessness to the extent that we don't see any positive potential when we trust God and try to remedy our wrongdoings. As explained above, the devil is so diligent in putting traps in so many places in our lives, our minds and emotions that prevent us from living each of our lives to the fullest. Mistakes cannot be avoided by any of us no matter how perfect we are.

> "To err is human." (Errare Humanum Est.)
> – Latin Proverb

What's crucial is to find the positive turning point in our mind by looking at the situation and what's done in a humble and earnest manner, truly repenting and resolving for the better while concurrently endeavoring to not being restrained by the unnecessary negative feelings of shame, fear, guilt or condemnation. Such balanced self-esteem is only possible when we are truly committed to God's plan for each of our lives and in turn we take courage and do our best to correct the wrongs, learn from it, improve ourselves and live in accordance of His love and plan for us.

## (5) Self-fulfilling Prophecy

Self-fulfilling prophecy is a subject in psychology highlighting the virtuous cycle of having faith in oneself and the positive result of such belief and conviction. Even if a person is not able to do something, if he or she keeps sending the message to oneself that he or she can do it, the result is more likely that the person can actually achieve it, rather than fail at it. If we focus on our mistakes, inadequacies, faults and external difficulties such as unfair socio-economic structure, barriers and obstacles, we are in essence sending a self-fulfilling prophecy toward a downward spiral, rather than an upward spiral. In my view, having faith in God and regularly attending church services and spending time to read bible and pray can be viewed as an effort to confirm a self-fulfilling prophecy to live a life as the precious child of God, making the fundamental transition from worldly or sinful addiction or dependency on temporary pleasures, to the ultimate faith in salvation, eternity and heaven that God has promised. In other words, while we are hopeless sinners with so many faults and failings, once we believe in Jesus Christ and become a Christian, we now have a new opportunity to live as a new creation and the best way to sustain a lifestyle as the children of God is to constantly listen to the message of hope and love as promised in the bible, praising and praying to God as often as possible. In a sense, worship is the essential manifestation of our endeavor to send a positive self-fulfilling prophecy for ourselves that we can conduct through our mind, body and spirit so that we can think, talk and act differently than before.

> "But you are a chosen people, a royal priesthood, a holy nation, a people belonging to God, that you may declare the praises of Him who called you out of darkness into His wonderful light." (1 Peter 2:9)

Therefore, some people may treat Christianity merely as one of the positive schools of psychology or mind control mechanisms or put it on the equal footing in line with various belief systems such as other religions like Buddhism or Taoism and academic or street-smart logical regime focusing on self-help, willpower, transcendence, nirvana or harmony.

However, Christianity is fundamentally different from other belief systems or academic subjects in that it is the only religion that presents the hope for the future based on the love of our savior, God and His specific plan and purpose for each of us. Only because there is a creator of universe who loves us unconditionally and wants to encourage us to live with a sense of purpose, we can overcome the unbelievable challenges in our lives relying on such promises. We should have the discernment and wisdom to know the fundamental difference that Christianity provides for our lives in dealing with our ultimate demise and, through that, it provides the incomparable solution to live our current lives in the positive manner and to the fullest extent.

Ted Kennedy was a strategist who achieved meaningful social and economic goals by working effectively with political opponents to enact laws no matter how imperfect they are so that they can be in place to be improved and supplemented over time down the road, rather than failing to put it in place due to the divergent differences in views in opposing political parties.

"Never let the perfect be the enemy of the good."
— Voltaire

It is far more efficient and necessary to send a positive self-fulfilling prophecy to ourselves that 'we can and should do better as a new creation', rather than being stigmatized by our faults, mistakes and weaknesses or being discouraged by unfortunate incidents and circumstances. And the ultimate, most powerful self-fulfilling prophecy in this world is to have the belief in God's promise towards us and accepting that promise as our own conviction to carry on with our lives to the best way possible. That is so much better than setting an unreachable goal, relying on our own efforts only, without trusting God and ultimately ending our lives in the event it doesn't work out as expected.

Only through the most powerful and effective self-fulfilling prophecy in the form of continued worship based on the Gospel and the promise of God, I sincerely hope we can continue the virtuous cycle of an upward spiral to live a better today than yesterday and a much better tomorrow than today.

# 7. The Greatest Power: Not Giving Up at This Moment

"Being Beaten is temporary. Quitting is permanent."

— Anonymous

### (1) Look Further

There are two insightful and inspiring fables involving chicken and eagle as follows[13]:

> "1 - The Eagle Who Thought He Was a Chicken: A baby eagle became orphaned when something happened to his parents. He glided down to the ground from his nest but was not yet able to fly. A man picked him up. The man

---

13) https://lifelessons4u.wordpress.com/tag/the-eagle-who-thought-he-was-a-chicken/

took him to a farmer and said, "This is a special kind of barnyard chicken that will grow up big." The farmer said, "Don't look like no barnyard chicken to me." "Oh yes, it is. You will be glad to own it." The farmer took the baby eagle and placed it with his chickens. The baby eagle learned to imitate the chickens. He could scratch the ground for grubs and worms too. He grew up thinking he was a chicken. Then one day an eagle flew over the barnyard. The eagle looked up and wondered, "What kind of animal is that? How graceful, powerful, and free it is." Then he asked another chicken, "What is that?" The chicken replied, "Oh, that is an eagle. But don't worry yourself about that. You will never be able to fly like that." And the eagle went back to scratching the ground. He continued to behave like the chicken he thought he was. Finally he died, never knowing the grand life that could have been his.

2 - Fable of the Eagle and the Chicken: A fable is told about an eagle who thought he was a chicken. When the eagle was very small, he fell from the safety of his nest. A chicken farmer found the eagle, brought him to the farm, and raised him in a chicken coop among his many chickens. The eagle grew up doing what chickens do, living like a chicken, and believing he was a chicken. A naturalist came to the chicken farm to see if what he had heard about an eagle acting like a chicken was really true. He knew that

an eagle is king of the sky. He was surprised to see the eagle strutting around the chicken coop, pecking at the ground, and acting very much like a chicken. The farmer explained to the naturalist that this bird was no longer an eagle. He was now a chicken because he had been trained to be a chicken and he believed that he was a chicken. The naturalist knew there was more to this great bird than his actions showed as he "pretended" to be a chicken. He was born an eagle and had the heart of an eagle, and nothing could change that. The man lifted the eagle onto the fence surrounding the chicken coop and said, "Eagle, thou art an eagle. Stretch forth thy wings and fly." The eagle moved slightly, only to look at the man; then he glanced down at his home among the chickens in the chicken coop where he was comfortable. He jumped off the fence and continued doing what chickens do. The farmer was satisfied. "I told you it was a chicken," he said. The naturalist returned the next day and tried again to convince the farmer and the eagle that the eagle was born for something greater. He took the eagle to the top of the farmhouse and spoke to him: "Eagle, thou art an eagle. Thou dost belong to the sky and not to the earth. Stretch forth thy wings and fly." The large bird looked at the man, then again down into the chicken coop. He jumped from the man's arm onto the roof of the farmhouse. Knowing what eagles are really about, the naturalist asked the farmer to let him try one more time. He would return the next day and prove that this bird was an eagle. The farmer, convinced otherwise, said, "It is a chicken." The naturalist returned the next morning to the chicken farm and took the eagle and the farmer some distance away to the foot of a high mountain. They could not see the farm nor the chicken coop from this new setting. The man held the eagle on his arm and pointed high into the sky where the bright sun was beckoning above. He spoke: "Eagle, thou art an eagle! Thou dost belong to the sky and not to the earth. Stretch forth thy wings and fly." This time the eagle stared skyward into the bright sun, straightened his large body, and stretched his massive wings. His wings moved, slowly at first, then surely and powerfully. With the mighty screech of an eagle, he flew. (In Walk Tall, You're A Daughter of God, by Jamie Glenn)"

The analogy is often made to chicken for people of small faith and eagle for faithful people. Chickens look to the ground most of the time seeking food and respond instantly depending on whether there is food going back and forth in a hasty, frivolous and changeable manner and such image is akin to those who lack in-depth faith to remain steady and patient even if the efforts don't result in immediate results. It appears that one of the reasons that chickens can't fly is because they stopped making use of their wings having lived for generations 'ground-based life'. This is why I think it can be so hard for us to think positively and 'heaven-oriented thinking' once we are accustomed to the 'ground-based thinking and lifestyle'. On the other hand, eagles are more stable and fly high above, instead of coming down back and forth in a flippant manner, looking over wide territory in a patient and sturdy posture. And we are all familiar with the image of eagle that the bible uses to encourage believers.

> "Do you not know? Have you not heard? The Lord is the everlasting God, the Creator of the ends of the earth. He will not grow tired or weary, and his understanding no one can fathom. He gives strength to the weary and increases the power of the weak. Even youths grow tired and weary, and young men stumble and fall; but those who hope in the Lord will renew their strength. They will soar on wings like eagles; they will run and not grow weary, they will walk and not be faint." (Isaiah 40:28-31)

We can further appreciate how believers are more akin to eagles when we meditate how we are ultimately upgraded at the instant we accept Jesus as our savior and we become the children of God who created the entire universe and who is still in control. If we are firmly rooted in the faith that we are granted with the authority and power to live our lives as a new creation in a new status of children of God, we can have the attitude and strength like that of an eagle and stop reacting instantly and frivolously to good and adverse events in life. We would be able to be more patient and have the capacity to endure in the face of the most unfortunate and challenging incidents in life because we have the strong conviction that God loves us no matter what and we will come out stronger and better in any given situation and furthermore we can love and respect our neighbors as we were loved by God unconditionally, helping others and sharing the good news of God's salvation and everlasting love toward us.

Are we reacting like chicken based on trivial calculation of plus and minus in dealing with the relationship with people around us, feeling uncomfortable around certain people who are different and not beneficial to us and frustrated that things don't work out immediately as we planned? Can we have some patience and long-term viewpoint like eagle in dealing with relationship problems in our lives?

There is an expression, "Take the high road" which signifies the importance of generosity and honorable character in dealing with negative people. For example, when someone is spreading false rumor about me, I can either respond in an equal manner to go around and tell people about his or her wrongdoing and lies, or I can take the high road like eagle and just focus on the things I need to do to live my life in a confident manner.

In my view, majority of people fall within the range of spectrum between two extreme categories – i.e., ones in one end of the spectrum who are capable of enduring the heaviest, unimaginable burdens that the life has to offer in the form of most hurtful scars and losses in life, deep-rooted secret that cannot be shared with anyone else but God and an unbearable sense of guilt that we carry for the rest of our lives for the things that we did in the past and the others on the other end of the spectrum who cannot even tolerate the tiniest problem or hardship and scream and vent out in desperation causing nuisance to people around them. I am confident that faith and hope in God is the ultimate source of power that enables the first category of people to live in such steadfast manner despite the substantial burdens of our lives and excruciating weight of our pain and suffering.

The naturalist who kept coming back to encourage the eagle in the farm is like God's image in my view in that God believes in our potential and continues to encourage us despite our ongoing doubts, ignorance and mistakes. God continually reminds us that we should live a 'heaven-based life', rather than 'ground-based life.' Perhaps the eagle was frustrated and upset when the naturalist finally took him to the mountain because he was out of his comfort zone and there probably was not food around that was readily available! But only then, the eagle was able to realize who he was and find ways to live his authentic life amid unfamiliar challenge and unique environment.

In the same manner, God is helping us in a mysterious manner and sometimes it is hard to understand why God has allowed some terrible things happened to us, but if we can remain persistent as eagle in our conviction in Him, not easily complaining and giving up, then we will one day find out that there was ultimately good plan for us through such happenings and we just needed to be more patient, more faithful and more positive no matter how difficult it may be at the time.

## (2) The Greatest Power is the Power to Not Give Up 'Right at This Moment'

When we are faced with unforeseen tragedy, failure, sickness, or loss of family, friends and people we love, we must go through a mourning period and allow ourselves to be restored waiting patiently to recover our strength in heart and mind to go on. The length of such mourning period would differ for each of us in that for some it could be an instant and for others it could last forever. What's important though is to not make any destructive decision out of frustration or deep sorrow to give up and let go during that period and remain constant in our faith in God. During that mourning period, it is crucial that we surrender our ego to the Almighty God, including our independent will, addiction to temporary distractions such as alcohol, drugs, or other undesirable pleasure-seeking activities, bad influences and reliance on untrustworthy people.

### All to Jesus, I Surrender

J. W. VanDeVenter and W. S. Weeden

All to Jesus I surrender, all to Him I freely give.
I will ever love and trust him, In His presence daily live.
All to Jesus I surrender, humbly at His feet I bow.
Worldly pleasures all forsaken, take me, Jesus, take me now.
All to Jesus I surrender; make me, Savior, wholly Thine.
Let me feel the Holy Spirit, truly know that Thy art mine.
All to Jesus I surrender, Lord, I give myself to Thee.
Fill me with Thy love and power, let Thy blessing fall on me.
All to Jesus I surrender; now I feel the sacred flame.
Oh, the joy of full salvation! Glory, glory, to His name!
Refrain: I surrender all, I surrender all, all to Thee,
    my blessed Savior, I surrender all.

This hymn is so beautiful in that it describes what we should do in our daily lives and when faced with incomprehensible difficulties. Only when we surrender our pride and ego, then Jesus can step in to help and guide us to the right direction towards ultimate deliverance. We are familiar with how Oprah shared her testimonial about this hymn that she desperately wanted to play the role of Sofia in the movie, The Color Purple in 1985 and auditioned for that role. She did her best, went on a diet and prayed so hard to be selected, but one day she was so troubled when she heard that another actress was being considered for that role and out of desperation, she decided to let go of her obsession and sang this hymn instead, giving her desires and disappointment to God. Later that day, there was a phone call from Steven Spielberg to notify her that she got that role and she couldn't even believe it happened. I am sure that she could never forget that day of surrendering to God and the miracle that He brought on to her.

All of us have unique experiences of such mysterious workings of God, requiring us to surrender first before He steps in. It is so easy to stay stubborn in our own thinking, ways that we are used to and stick with the pattern of negative thinking and give in to the temptations of wrong paths and temporary distractions, and in particular it is so easy to feel discouraged when terrible things happen to us. However, we should have the strength in our heart to stay positive by surrendering our pain and suffering to God in order to experience the unbelievable miracle and blessing that He has in store for us, even when it seems that giving up and staying negative is the only way. During the mourning period of our lives, let us have the patience to endure for some time until we are restored, seeking His help in a humble mind. The expression, "Time heals everything" denotes the importance of endurance and we are familiar with the story of King Solomon who asked for the wisest of the world to gather up all the wisdom and come out with a single advice that provides the ultimate consolation in the deepest moment of sadness and pain, and they inscribed "This too shall pass" in that ring of wisdom.

The easiest thing to do when it's hard is of course giving up and going down the downward spiral. However, the most important power we need amid worst possible scenario is to not give up right at that moment when the temptation to do so is so powerful and irresistible. While remaining calm and steadfast during crisis, I suggest we divert our attention to finding different ways to look at the current situation by opening ourselves to the trustworthy people, relying on faith and promises in the bible, praying, praising and meditating on God's words, and quietly going on with our lives in the most optimistic way possible. And even when we realize that there is no one who can be trusted with our pain and agony, then perhaps we could resolve to become that trustworthy person to those who need encouragement, consolation and support based on the firm faith in God and His words.

Pastor Hyun-soo Lim was held captivate in North Korea for two and a half years from 2015 until the unexpected release in August 2017, serving a life sentence and living prison camp forced to do hard labor for no reason other than trying to do some humanitarian work there and evangelize North Koreans. In one of his testimonials, he stated that while he was free from fear through the grace of God, he struggled with extreme loneliness since he had eaten 2,757 meals all by himself as he was in solitary confinement. He said he spent the remaining time, other than the forced labor, reading and memorizing the bible and hymns and reading those books that were permitted by the authority. I could feel God's providence and love when he was miraculously rescued by the Canadian government's efforts, seeing how great a human being he is for having such incredibly strong courage and faith in God under such extremely appalling circumstances.

Let us have a strong will and firm attitude like an eagle based on an unyielding faith in God to enable us to daringly say 'No' to the negative thoughts that come into our mind as soon as we wake up in the morning every day or whenever we are faced with difficulty, remembering to be thankful to the parts of our body that perform their respective roles to sustain ourselves no matter how hurt, sad, upset or disappointed we are. That power to make a small constructive choice willfully in resistance to the temptation of destructive thinking every day and every moment and in the face of obstacles and difficulties is the essence of the 'authentic power' that each of us possesses no matter how insignificant a choice it may seem. And the source of ultimate power to enable such genuine power is our steadfast faith in God that is not comparable to any other belief systems in this world.

PART II

# What to do

# 8.
# Have Faith

## (1) Faith in God

We all need encouragement when faced with difficulty so that we can see the light at the end of tunnel, and the most reliable source of encouragement is our God. The word, encouragement is made up of 'en' (to make it possible from outside) and 'courage', and I suggest that we rely on the help from God, not just focus on ourselves and our will because His help is the most powerful and reliable source available in this world. As I have realized from a small incident in Singapore observing a container-like thing being pulled forcefully by the crane on top of the high-rise building to be delivered from the precarious condition when it was in hanging by the line, God is the source of the ultimate power who can deliver us out of our predicaments.

In contrast, I shared in earlier parts how suicide is synonymous with self-deliverance, which is an attempt to deliver ourselves on our own. Human beings have the amazing machine called the 'brain' that is superior to any sophisticated computers in some way which enables independent thinking and information processing. However, our brains are like a double-edged sword in that when working properly it is so beneficial, but once it is corrupted with inaccurate information or is erroneously programmed, then we are inevitably caged by our own thoughts and false analysis. Human beings are the only animals who can deliberately undertake self-destructive behaviors, limiting the options to just give up and end it all when the difficulties seem unbeatable, while there are plenty of other alternatives out there that could improve the impending problems in the long run.

> "See to it that no one falls short of the grace of God and that no bitter root grows up to cause trouble and defile many." (Hebrews 12:15)

Most of our daily happenings are opportunities that could make us better or bitter, ultimately in the latter's case, leading us to grow bitter roots within ourselves that manifest in our negative attitude, mindset and behaviors. Once we make a choice in one direction, there will be added force to such an upward or downward spiral for the weight of our choices accumulates over time. No matter how hard it is to overcome skepticism that lures us to reject the Gospel and no matter how strong the force of enticement toward a pessimistic way of viewing things and losing hope, we should be so determined in being deeply rooted in faith, and I would like to share four important characteristics of Christianity that I think are of most essential based on my experiences in life to date.

First, Christianity in my view is the religion that gives true, unconditional 'second chance' in our lives based on the ultimate salvation. In society, it is so easy to be stigmatized once you make one mistake and it is hard to have a true second chance once a relationship is ruined. All of us make mistakes and what's important is to repent, learn from it and resolve to not repeat it going forward having faith and hope in ourselves based on the promise of God no matter how disparaging the conditions are. However, the devil uses our mistakes and inadequacies as traps to enchain us to condemnation focusing only on such negative attributes of ourselves and forgetting the promises and love of God. The devil keeps sending the discouraging messages like, you can't be helped, you were born like this, you can never get better, you are not lucky, there is no plan or dream for you and the like.

> "Therefore, if anyone is in Christ, the new creation has come; the old has gone, the new is here." (2 Corinthians 5:17)

However, God gives us the opportunity to live a completely transformed life as soon as we choose faith and accept Jesus as our savior so that we become the children of God at that moment. Therefore, we now have the authority and power to overcome our previous ways, old habits and negative tendencies and live the life of light and blessing based on the promises of God. Even when we revert back to our old selves repeating our mistakes and unhealthy habits despite the rebirth, God never gives up and grants us another chance to start over and do it better. That's why I earnestly seek to find the presence of God in my life whenever I am filled with defeat and guilt over missteps and failures pressed down by the heavy burden of doubt so that the darkness in me is overtaken by the powerful force of light that is God.

Second, Christianity teaches us what 'true freedom' is and gives it unconditionally. Without God, we can never be entirely free from various restraints in our lives. Our starting point is restrained from the very beginning in that, even those who call out 'My Way Only', we could not and did not choose our parents and where we were born. I don't remember if I chose to be born in Korea. Some philosophers state that we are 'thrown into' our family at the time of birth and we live our lives according to what's given at the beginning. Some may feel fortunate for having been born into a rich and perfect family, some may resent for the predicament in poverty and mistreatment; furthermore, through the course of our lives, something bad happens and we may unfortunately be gripped by such event in that we cannot have the freedom to truly enjoy and live our lives.

Living the life as slaves is unbelievably painful destiny in that our existence, dignity and value is entirely under the control of the master and we have no power over our own life. But sometimes we volunteer to become slaves without even being aware. For instance, we may start liking something like smartphone, alcohol, video games, drugs, shopping and many other things in life because they are attractive, fun, useful or cool at the beginning; but, over time we realize that we become addicted to the harmful level and we feel anxious without it. The true solution that helps us to overcome any form of addiction or undesirable dependency can be found only when we know the true salvation that comes from God.

> "Then, you will know the Truth, and the Truth will set you free." (John 8:32)

Only when we fully appreciate God's love and plan for us, we can genuinely be free from all the emotional and psychological traps in life that are placed by the devil to enslave us into addiction, damaging emotions like anger, disappointment, resentment, fear, doubt and loneliness. God loves us so much that He sent His only son to die on the cross for us to reconnect with Him so that we can be the children of God. Once we understand the extent of His love and grace, we then can see the immeasurable freedom and boundless hope that lie in front of us purely because of His ineffable love and indescribable grace extended to us.

> "I am the Way and Truth and the Life. No one comes to the Father except through Me." (John 14:6)

If we found Jesus, we have found the way, truth and the life itself.

In turn, this suggests, without Jesus, we will be confused, deceived and living half-life. Belief in Jesus is equivalent to obtaining the mysterious key to the inexhaustible potential that provides an ultimate solution to small and big problems, establishes essential core of our existences that sustains the critical balance in our lives, grants absolute freedom from all things that confined and enslaved us before, and enables a completely fresh start of our lives as a new creation, fundamentally transformed into a new person as our spirit is wholly renewed with the Holy Spirit. Let us not be bound and restricted by our regrettable old ways of life, irreparable missteps and regrets; but, rather stay humble and grateful to God for providing us with such wonderful key to all our problems and pains, and, therefore, take the bold step of faith into the world to open the seemingly formidable doors of the present and the future. And each of our steps going forward from there will continue to be sustained, encouraged and supported by the grace of God if we hold onto our faith and consciously make small and big choices in reliance of such steadfast faith, rather than our own thoughts, analysis and calculation, and we would be able to have the tremendous power and courage in our heart to overcome any obstacles or challenges in our lives.

My mom is the 16th generation descendant of General Jong-Seo Kim, whose courage and leadership during Chosun Dynasty is well documented by historians, but she grew up in a poor family and her parents decided to send her to an orphanage nearby during junior high to guarantee her high school education (which was rare for women to go to high school at that time) while she helps with chores and administrative duties. However, it seemed that the principal of that orphanage siphoned most of donations and provided the bare minimum essentials to the children. For instance, she told me one day that in most days the kids ate watery porridge made with old, bug-infested rice with aged radish soaked in salt (instead of more costly kimchi) but she said in a nostalgic manner, "Oh that watery porridge was so delicious somehow at that time…", and never expresses sadness or resentment about such miserable memories or the unethical principal. My mom, through faith, is completely free from blame, anger or hatred towards the abusive and unjust people or circumstance.

My dad is the same. Apparently when he lost his eyesight, he could distinguish light and dark to a certain extent, but he went to a prayer house in a rural area and went on a few 30 day fasting prayers. One day, he was so thirty to the extent that he felt that his body was burning up, so begged for a glass of water to wet his mouth but the female principal of that place kicked the glass that my dad was holding. My dad said after those repeated fasting prayers, he completely lost his eyesight, but he was somehow overjoyed with confidence that he now found the way to live a life of a blind person because he found Jesus Christ. My dad never said negative things about that incident but it's just that I heard from other people or read it in his book and I felt so upset about what happened. Furthermore, even in terms of people around us that I think are rude, inappropriate or selfish and share my sentiment of disappointment to my parents, they always tell me to look at their positives, humbly reflect on myself and consider others better than myself. In sum, they live in the state of phenomenal freedom from any emotional affliction from people, environment and incidents, based on their ultra-strong faith and commitment to God. And, their examples always remind me that I should live my life based on the unqualified priority in life, surrendering my ego to God and His grace to experience the full extent of true freedom.

Third, Christianity prompts me to choose 'life', instead of death, and stay 'positive' no matter what based on the love of God.

> "But I trust in Your unfailing love; my heart rejoices in Your salvation." (Psalm 13:5)

This relates to the resurrection of Jesus and the eternal life we have after death. Even at the point of ultimate death, it's not a tragic ending but rather a beginning of the unbelievably beautiful life that we cannot even imagine. Therefore, it is the essential core of the positivity that even the force of darkness and death cannot inhibit, and that's why I argue "Each of our lives is A BCDE". And only on the basis of such faith and perspective on lives, we can live our present lives in an unreservedly positive manner, obediently and faithfully bearing our pain and tears no matter how tough and hard it may be, deeply trusting and hoping for heaven where there is no tear and no pain, and, furthermore, we can live a generous lifestyle sharing with and loving our neighbors because we now have such a big heart that is so free and so grateful for the love of God for us, and as light shines reaching out to the darkest corners, we also live the lives of true light.

> "The thief comes only to steal, kill and destroy. I have come that they may have life, and have it to the full." (John 10:10)

If we are absorbed in our narrow-mindedness and lopsided thinking, we become easy targets of the thieves and the devil who steal our life, joy, happiness and gratitude, using the tools of negative emotions like self-doubt, blame, fear, resentment, loneliness and self-hatred based on our own mistakes, some unfortunate incidents or socio-economic barriers. The thief steals our healthy self-esteem and destroys the potential to live peacefully, joyfully and in harmony with others, sharing God's love toward us. Initially, such thieves approach us in the sweetest way possible as if they are on our side comforting and helping us to feel better, so it is so crucial that we have the discernment to distinguish such forces of devil who approaches in such enticing manner vis-à-vis the true helping hands of God that sometimes feel so far away when we lose sight of its importance due to the secular lifestyle, negative thoughts and undesirable emotions.

As stated earlier, the term, suicide is synonymous with self-deliverance, and it essentially signifies our independent attempt to save ourselves when we are deceived by the devil who insidiously steal our self-esteem and freedom using emotional traps. Such extreme manifestation of self-deliverance shows the eventual downside of our attempts to help and deliver ourselves vis-à-vis the importance of true deliverance that comes from God. When we are delivered, we are completely free and loved and we can't just commit such acts of destruction. Rather, we love ourselves and further step out to share His love with others with such kindness and grace, and we can't possibly be cold, cynical, skeptical or rude towards other people because there is unbelievable warmth in those true Christians that cannot be found in ordinary people based on mysterious and thoughtful consideration and generosity that covers all sins.

I visited London for training and work back in 2006 or 07, and happened to see the puppet musical, 'Avenue Q'. The synopsis is the lead puppet, Princeton graduated with a degree in English literature, but has a tough time finding a job and a place to stay. Depressed and gloomy, he finds a small room in the corner of Avenue Q in a shared house with other puppets who are mostly defeated and not-so-successful. Princeton and other roommates one day sing "It sucks to be me!" lamenting on their lives, but in the end Princeton finds the purpose and meaning in life helping others using his experiences. It's such a comical and enjoyable masterpiece, which is also inspiring in many ways. I remember one scene when Princeton shares his disappointment that he now realizes he is not that special even though his parents told him so and he could do anything when he was a little kid, his cute roommates, the 'Bad Idea Bears, two charming troublemakers' respond 'yes, you are right!', which throws audience a big laugh because it is just so unexpected, and the bears had no intention to encourage him whatsoever. When Princeton receives some money from his parents, these Bad Idea Bears sincerely advise him to spend it on beers.

While these two cute bears provided laughter and some release as it was just such a witty way for people to realize that you really should not go to that direction of destructive thinking, there are many not-so-cute, rather horrible people with bad intention who want to destroy our will to go on and crush strength of heart to overcome the daily obstacles of our lives. People advise their kids to hang out with 'right friends', because adults appreciate how important to have the right people around when you are in difficulties and desolation. Those people around us can drive us up or down in susceptible moments with a single word, one hug or one loving gaze or, sadly, one corrupted advice or misguided counsel.

In this regard, I want to emphasize the importance of finding trustworthy people. We do need someone who can listen to us and help us, but we need to know whether the person has a deep faith with a trustworthy and reliable character. Just because someone has a certain status, we should not just assume as such. I want to sincerely congratulate those who have found such people but if we are disappointed and hurt because some people turned out to be the opposite, using our hurt and pain to take advantage of us or spreading bad rumors, then still don't lose heart and trust in God to make it right and never lose hope that we will meet the right people. Moreover, it is also possible that we now make a determination to be that trustworthy person who sincerely helps and wishes for the best for the people around us as faithful Christians. I believe those good-hearted Christians should work together to make this place better against the forces of darkness and evil. The bible is clear that the thieves came to steal, kill and destroy whereas Jesus has come to let us have life to the full. Once we have found Jesus, we have His power and love on our side within ourselves to enable us to be the true force of love and graciousness toward ourselves as well as others so that we could truly live to the full. Therefore, no matter how doomed the reality seems at this stage, we really need to just surrender our prejudice and lopsided thinking and boldly take the step of faith to choose God and the hope that is in Him.

Fourth, Christianity provides 'vision and direction' for our lives to live as the children of God, as a new creation, enjoying complete freedom and rejoicing each day in a positive manner, and ultimately, to love our neighbors as our own. True Christians cannot be selfish, cold, mean or live an ego-centric lifestyle; rather, carry on with the life with true humility, love, commitment and sacrifice.

> "Do nothing out of selfish ambition or vain conceit. Rather, in humility value others above yourselves, not looking to your own interests but each of you to the interests of the others." (Philippians 2:3)

This is something I frequently observed from my parents. My mom is overly humble and considerate for others and usually only takes the marginal parts of any food that people usually don't like to eat, for instance, offering freshest parts of fruits and main body parts of fish while she would take the old, top or bottom part only, and does not hesitate to give the best food available at home to the visitors. I haven't seen anyone like my mom through my life-long experience of going to churches in a few countries to date who so sincerely respects others like that, and I am always challenged in that regard as well in that I am not like that either in many ways. Shamefully, of course I want the good parts, if not the best, and it takes a lot of sacrificial heart to offer the best parts to someone else, come to think about it. However, my mom has lived like that throughout her life always giving the best parts to my dad, me and my siblings. I actually became somewhat indifferent to that pattern of behavior over time, but my husband one day told me that he found it a bit odd that she always gives all the freshest seafood and good parts to my dad while she eats only the leftovers when we eat together because such scene was quite foreign to him.

So nowadays I sometimes criticize my mom that she should eat decent food instead of giving them all to my dad and ourselves, but she just says that she finds the parts she eats delicious. I honestly don't understand the extent of her sacrificial heart sometimes, but at the same time fully appreciate that her attitude is exemplary of true Christian humbleness and sacrifice. Also, she intentionally picks somewhat damaged fruits in the market while I do my best to find the best quality checking every corner, and I asked her why she would be so silly, and she said, "The owner should be able to sell these also, not just the good ones, to have a viable business…" Her attitude makes me feel embarrassed at times and question whether I am too selfish. I one day asked her how she endured the challenging times accompanying my dad when the people didn't treat the blind very kindly back in 1970s and 80s, but she just responded that, "Why do you ask such thing, and it was no problem at all…" and quietly turns her eyes back to her bible that she was reading at the time. My dad is also quite inspiring in that while he is so close to retirement, he still does various voluntary works to provide acupuncture treatment and free food to the old people in rural area around Daejeon to evangelize them at some point and to visit various social welfare centers to preach on a regular basis, in addition to providing financial support.

Reflecting on these examples of my parents' somewhat overly-stubborn and hard-to-understand lifestyle, I ask, "What am I doing with the talents and blessings that I got as the child of God to serve Him and to spread the good news, as commanded by God?" It is true that just living my own life well and for my own happiness in this competitive world is hard enough and we are all so busy keeping up with the Joneses in some way and I in most cases am driven to just focus on my life, like other people seem to do. But, because I know that I should live as the salt and light of this world as the child of God, I also think about the ultimate direction of life and what God's vision is for my life, having generously given me certain talents and unique experiences. Taking one step further, I at times think about what I would feel most proud at the time of my ultimate demise and what comes to my mind are those various images of my parents who lived so honorably in comparison with my self-centered lifestyle most of the times. I truly believe God has made me my parents' daughter to witness what it means to organize our lives based on the absolute priority committed to God in this world, and in that regard, I am eternally grateful for God's salvation and love for me to deliver me from my distraction, disbelief or doubts that could have rejected any hint of Gospel without the extraordinary living examples of true Christians right in front of my nose.

### (2) Have Faith in You (Self-Esteem)

Once we have faith in God and His love for us, we naturally begin to have faith in His plan and purpose for our lives as well.

That faith in Him and ourselves are like two sides of one coin. It's inevitable that we have faith and confidence in us precisely because we believe in God, and that's the essential component of positivity based on the Christian faith. Such faith and self-esteem cannot be proud, flawed or reckless over-confidence or arrogance. Rather, we are fully cognizant of our ineptness as sinner without Him, but because of our belief in Jesus, we are called to be the children of God with a clear purpose in this life to be the meaningful, hopeful and wonderful people we are, and we live each day full of confidence, hope and positive attitude.

> "I can do all this through Him who gives me strength."
>
> (Philippians 4:13)

Those who are humble and yet so confident in themselves are the ones with a balanced 'self-esteem', which is commonly defined as follows:

> "Self-esteem reflects a person's overall subjective emotional evaluation of his or her own worth. It is a judgment of oneself as well as an attitude toward the self. Self-esteem encompasses beliefs about oneself (for example, "I am competent", "I am worthy"), as well

as emotional states, such as triumph, despair, pride, and shame." (Wikipedia[14])

This self-esteem should be approached in a cautious manner, because without such caution, we can easily fall into over-confidence or arrogance that is out of balance and undesirable. Those who have ideal self-esteem will never be able to think that they are better than others just because they are Christians or of some status in this society; rather, they respect others as much as they respect themselves. It's a mysterious symbiosis and balance in our heart and attitude, and that's why I think it is so rare to find someone with such honorable self-esteem even if there are millions of Christians who claim to be believers.

> "Without God, we cannot; without us, He will not."
> – Augustine.

Why did God ask us to do our part spreading His words and be the examples in this world, when He can just do it all by Himself? After all, He is the creator of the universe and He did it all at that time. However, with the plan to deliver us from evil and hopeless

---
14) https://en.wikipedia.org/wiki/Self-esteem

destiny, He gave us certain circumstances and incomprehensible events and happenings, arranged to meet up with certain people that we would rather not meet and gave us freedom and right to choose and react. Many questions can arise like why God leaves the darkness prevail in this world and why bad things happen to good people. However, no matter how strong the temptation is to keep querying, doubting and rejecting, if we choose God in the thickest clouds of skepticism and anguish, I am convinced that God unquestionably encourages us, answers our questions, doubts and agonies and ultimately helps and delivers us therefrom, leading us to the path of salvation and eternity. It is true that without God, we can't do that much. When things look grim and we lose hope in our work, relationship and ourselves, there isn't much we can do, and it is so easy to give up and just let go. However, when we choose God and act on it, despite hopelessness and impediments, we have the invaluable chance to witness how God works miracle in things that seem so impossible and unlikely.

**I am light. - India Arie**

I am light, I am light. I am not the things my family did. I am not the voices in my head. I am not the pieces of the brokenness inside.

I am light, I am light. I'm not the mistakes that I have made, Or any of the things that caused me pain. I am not the pieces of the dream I left behind.

I am light, I am light. I am not the color of my eyes. I am not the skin on the outside. I am not my age, I am not my race, my soul inside is all light.

All light, all light. I am light, I am light. I am the divinity defined. I am the God on the inside. I am a star, a piece of it all. I am light.

I understand that India made this song when she was going through a major crisis as a musician at some point and it is such an inspiring piece. This song reminds me to realize that God's light comes through the cracks in our lives shedding the powerful light through the scars and wounds that we carry due to our failed relationship, repetitive and reckless actions, rushed decisions, regrettable blunders, and lots of emotional and psychological baggage we carry around. And only when we fully accept that formidable light from God, then we become one with that light so that we can feel, think, act and talk like that light in resemblance of God, the Father of our lives.

## (3) Respect Others

If we truly believe in God, we inevitably have a balanced self-esteem that believes in and respect ourselves as well as others. It is unavoidable for the light to hide or draw a line on its light that shines, and it always brightens up around itself. We can't resolve to live as a light while not influencing others in a positive way. As long as we are light, we naturally influence others in a profound manner. It's hard to draw boundaries as to how far that light goes. That's why we do not sincerely believe in God if we turn our back against other people who need help and encouragement, if we maintain coldness and nonchalance towards other people and if we are not sympathetic with others' pain and suffering.

Those who have faithfully complied with the religious commands of Christianity, going to morning services every day, tithing, reading bible and regimentally praying each day can easily fall into the delusion that they are the best kinds of Christians and those are the only things that matter without taking into account how their arrogance based on religious act actually damages other people's perception of true Christianity and how their lack of humility and kind compassion undermines the possibility to have a deeply intimate relationship with God and people around them. Arrogant believers who don't reflect on their lifestyle and attitude can almost never inspire any one. There is a saying that, "People believe in the same way as their character or personality," which means that selfish people use faith to live selfish, power-hungry people will use belief to control others, and resentful people use religion to vent out their anger and justify their character or personality. God is so powerful in that He will even change the inherent flaws in our character once we are truly committed, but if we remain a superficial or formalistic believer, that fundamental transformation will never happen because it is just so difficult to change our personality. I also try my best to change my undesirable personality, but I fully appreciate it is a life-long work-in-progress and always endeavor to remember that I need to work on so many imperfections and inadequacies in order to live as the rightful child of God.

> "Humility is the fear of the Lord; its wages are riches and honor and life." (Proverbs 22:4)

Humility is equivalent to the fear of the Lord, the bible says. As long as we remain arrogant and proud, we are not respecting God and we would not be able to live our lives in a wise and prudent manner, because wisdom can only be found in the humble heart. We have so much respect if somebody is successful and amazing and yet modest at the same time, but if we find out that the person is arrogant and proud for his or her achievement, the attraction and appeal disappear. We have become like kings and queens once we believe in God as the children of God, but only with true humility and humbleness that fully appreciates and acknowledges that we were once hopeless sinners in the darkest pit of misery and distress, and yet God so loved us unconditionally and delivered us from there, our light can genuinely shine inside and outside ourselves, illuminating His indescribable grace and love through ourselves.

# 9.
# Find True Motives

## (1) Why Do I Want This

I believe we need to have true motives for the direction of our lives we choose in each milestone including our occupation in order to overcome any obstacles along the way. Just because it looks good, it pays well, other people say it's good, or it's easy do not constitute true motives. We need to have a serious reason for things that we choose and follow because without that we would always be tempted to give up even at the smallest obstacles that come in the way. As mentioned earlier, everyone, including 'the baddest man on the earth,' Mike Tyson wants the same thing, which is to live our lives well. However, what's different is what constitutes 'living well' to each of us and how to do it. So, while it is understandable that we all want to live well, we need to find ways to live well in a beneficial manner.

It is somewhat embarrassing to share this story, but I have had a problem since young that I never had any specific dream for my life. I remember when I was about 6-7 years old, I joined a lunch outing with my parents and other blind pastors at a restaurant. While I could sense the cold treatment offered by the restaurant owner and servers for having so many blind customers, I was stunned when we came out and the owner scattered salts on the ground at the entrance of the restaurant. I asked my mom why he did that, and my mom (or someone else) explained in essence, "Some people consider blind as unlucky and they sprinkle salt to get rid of unluckiness and mainly it's because of their prejudice and superstition." When I heard that, I felt very hurt and, at the same time, deep compassion for the blind people for being treated with such humiliation just because they are physically handicapped, despite that they could be actually better people than, for example, those restaurant owner and servers. Despite the physical disability, they may be more inspiring, smarter and more capable people with profound character and life philosophy, but just because they are physically limited, the fact that they were treated as such from certain people just seemed wrong even at that age. I remember at that time I told my parents that, "I want to marry a blind person when I grow up and help him," and my parents complemented that I was a good girl. In other words, I had a vague sense of wanting to help the weak and vulnerable in our society, but I just did not have any ambition or goal for my life.

In some way I blame my parents for this lack of ambition because my parents never told me or my siblings that we should be successful in life or go to good university or anything like that. They always said we should go to church, do offering, pray and read bible but never highlighted the importance of secular success. They asked us to study hard in obedience to God's command to work hard and during weekdays, study is what students do while on Sunday we should obey God and serve Him. But I always liked books and was an okay student but sometimes if I do very well, my parents were happy and that motivated me to study harder and I guess I somewhat felt proud and superior when I did well at school, which must have encouraged me to study hard.

During high school, I remember I realized one day that we study to go to a good university and up to that point, I honestly didn't know why we study because my parents never told me that I should go to a good university. Since then, I studied really hard to go to a university in Seoul, and thankfully I could. In terms of the major, I discussed with my parents and they wanted me to be a teacher or professor because I liked reading so I decided to major in Education. After graduating from university, I married my husband at the age of 25 because I felt that he was a good and trustworthy man and spent a few years before I finally decided to continue my education in graduate school in Canada. While I was finalizing a Master's thesis with the natural course to continue with a Doctoral Degree in the same department, I started to question whether I really want to remain in academia in the area of critical study. In essence, I felt that critical perspective based on social inequity that I was majoring in conflicts with my belief system focusing on the positive attitude based on Christianity.

In particular, I remember taking classes with Dr. Dorothy E Smith, based on her book entitled, "The Everyday World as Problematic: A Feminist Sociology", and it was such an honor because it was one of the last terms that she lectured before her impending retirement. I truly appreciated the critical viewpoints taught in her classes, but I somehow felt that those critical views pinpoint problems but do not provide any practical, helpful solutions. So, I kept thinking about what I wanted out of my life, and ultimately realized that I just did not know. Then, I decided to change the question and asked whether there is anything that I could do for others, for those who matter. That's when I remembered that deep in my heart I had this desire to be a lawyer for my dad, who really wanted to be a lawyer when he was young, but whose dream was cut short because of his sudden disability. I thought that there are a few characters of mine that are congruent with those of a lawyer, such as love of reading, thinking critically and analytically. So, with the courage of heart, I told my husband that, "I wanted to take the Law School Admission Test (LSAT) instead of just continuing with a doctoral degree", and he was quite surprised to hear such a sudden proposal and yet always supportive, he said, "Go ahead and give it a try, if that's what you want to do," because he, later shared, thought that it wouldn't work out anyways. So, while I was finalizing my Master's thesis, I registered for the LSAT prep school nearby and prepared concurrently. Some parts of the LSAT were easy but some were not, and yet I did not give up and the test scores were surprisingly quite high, and I got accepted to UBC law school in 2002. At that time, I was so surprised that I got admitted and it felt like God was happy with my decision to do something meaningful for his faithful servant, and it made me feel really good also. Since then, while there were ups and downs, I graduated from UBC law school with excellent GPAs and was hired by one of the biggest law firms in Canada for their articling program with a signing bonus and academic scholarship even before I started working and I became a lawyer in July 2006.

Through my humble experiences so far, one of the important things that I would like to underscore is to look at the "The Everyday World as Possibility" based on the Christian faith and positive mindset, rather than seeing "The Everyday World as Problematic", and while everything is possible, it is most important that we have the right reason and motive to want and do something. Once you have decided on the reason and have the right motive, then we should never give up in the face of so many challenges and obstacles, and continue to do our best. Ultimately, I shared my story above because I wanted to show how I found my motive based on what I could do for someone I cared when I could not decide on what I wanted, in the hope that I could help someone in a similar situation going through the agonies of not knowing what to do in life. It is somewhat humiliating that I did not know what I wanted but it is a risk worth taking if I could help at least one person out there who is frustrated with the fact that he or she does not have any strong passion for anything in this world. If you have a strong passion and drive for something specific, I truly congratulate, and I hope you achieve your dream. But even if you don't know what you want out of your life, I want to encourage to never give up hope and keep on looking inside and around as there must be something or some way that you can make meaningful difference in someone else's life if you just pay attention. The most important thing, of course, is to find the plan God has for you, and never give up on that faith once you've found it.

## (2) Stay Humble

At 9am on Friday, July 21, 2006, I attended the call to the bar ceremony at Roy Thomson Hall in Toronto, Ontario, and the keynote speaker, The Honorable Patrick J. Lesage Q.C. said something in essence to suggest the following in his speech:

> "You are not an important person, but you have an important role to play."

That statement left an indelible mark on my mind because I actually became a lawyer without any specific intent, for instance, to be a world-renowned international lawyer or to make a lot of money or to be a humanitarian lawyer who helps the weak or vulnerable; rather, I was an accidental lawyer who (although there was God's plan) became a lawyer through God's grace and love as He looked favorably at my wishes to do something meaningful for my dad and myself as well. However, that statement for whatever reason spoke to me in that although it's okay I don't have huge ambition or specific objective in life, I still can make difference and exert good influence as long as I never give up and stay humble. His advice felt like it was based on Christian faith in that we are worthless and hopeless without God, but if we accept Jesus Christ as our Savior, we are a new person and we can do anything and shine through the darkness through His power.

Furthermore, this statement and encouragement does not just apply to those people who were called to the bar that day. I truly believe that we all can live our best lives if we take this into our heart and trust that we can make a difference through the things we do in our lives. Everybody ultimately wants 'validation' about his or her life as it is coming close to the end that he or she has lived a good, valid and valuable life irrespective of whether it was a success or failure. As long as we have never given up, did our best and made a difference in someone's life, I believe we have lived well, and further, it would be quite fulfilling if there are some aspects in our lives that others could also evaluate that we have lived well despite many trials and errors. Most importantly, if our lives can be validated in the eyes of God by having lived our lives truly led by the Holy Spirit despite the ups and downs, lots of mistakes and failings, that would be the perfectly validated life with the seal of eternal approval because we know that we would be granted with the opportunity to enjoy the mysterious, unimaginable and exquisitely beautiful another world of eternity.

At times, I was disheartened by the fact that I did not know what I wanted to do in my life as I believed that having a passion for something would definitely help me live enthusiastically and with so much energy. One day, I saw an interview of Jane Goodall, an anthropologist and chimpanzee expert, and what shocked me was the statement she made, "At the age of nine, I knew exactly what I wanted to do in my life. I wanted to study chimpanzees for the rest of my life." I felt such huge distance between her and me in that I was a hopeless person who doesn't know what to do and sometimes I almost hated myself comparing with her who had such clear conviction at the age of nine! At any rate, I have so much respect for her that she had that passion and she committed her life to the study of chimpanzees for the entire life up to now living in the remote forest of Africa for the most part of her life. However, for those people out there who are like me, easy to be disappointed and lose heart because they don't have passion, I want to tell them that, "It's okay if you don't know what you want out of your life or if you feel disoriented. Just be patient and pray and look around yourself. It will come." Doing our best to know ourselves and to appreciate that we were made by God with a specific plan even if it's not clear to us right now and never losing hope to find that mission and calling in our lives will ultimately lead us to the right path. And now that I am over 40 having studied and worked in various fields, I would like to make three suggestions for those who feel unclear in terms of what to do.

First, I suggest we should follow our 'curiosity' if we don't have clear ambition or objective. It is to change the question from 'what should I do' to 'what am I interested in'. Someone said long time ago most people actually collect one thing in lives consistently, such as coins, clothes, shoes, postages, arts, cigars or whatever it may be. Similarly, there must be something that we are interested in and feel curious to know more about, and if we focus on that area, then something specific will come one day to guide us to the concrete career. Second, if there is anything 'meaningful' amongst the things I can do and achieve, then choose that. In my case, I chose to do something meaningful for my dad which was beneficial for me as it was an achievement for me also and amid confusion and ignorance on what I wanted out of my life, I changed my question from 'what do I want' to 'is there anything that I can do for the people I care about.' Third, to the extent possible, try to find the work you 'like'. Of course, I had a good motive and in some way, I am truly blessed but in the core of what happened was that there was something I really liked, which was English. As a non-native speaker of English, I started liking English since I started learning alphabet at junior high, and studying law was not so difficult because it was in English that I liked.

Looking back, I now wonder how many of us can have such exceptional conviction on our lives at such early age like Jane. Perhaps most of us don't have passion for something and still continue to live for various reasons, and maybe some of us aren't fortunate enough to even have the luxury of wondering what we want in our lives due to the practical barriers like poverty, abuse or other types of inconceivable hardships in life. Furthermore, I no longer feel inferior to her for not knowing what I want specifically and at times laugh at myself thinking how I can't imagine living in a forest in Africa surrounded by chimpanzees without Wi-Fi or other conveniences no matter how I actually prefer nature to city, and I am in some way grateful that such a strong conviction did not come to me to lead me to that direction. I hope we all have the room to find humor in our problems and agonies no matter how painful it is, comforting and encouraging ourselves that, 'It is okay as is and we just should go on and never give up, staying positive and staying humble.'

### (3) The Problem of Extremization of Motives

I don't think the over-competition for success is desirable perhaps because I never had that kind of competitive ambition or drive. Equally undesirable is the hopelessness or lethargy that lead to self-destructive life style wasting one's life potential. Just trying to be a number one or go to the top universities without specific intent on what we want in life or understanding on what we are truly good at and what is meaningful might lead to unhealthy competition and disorientation in the end. In contrast, easily giving up without even trying, focusing only on the socio-economic barriers, imperfections and inadequacies in ourselves and environment is not ideal either. What's critical and essential is to believe in God's plan for us and to believe in our potential so that we can do our best no matter what.

I lived and worked around Daechi-dong area in Gangnam, Seoul where it was filled with lots of academic institutions, and one stretch of long street is known as the 'education street'. One night I passed by the education street around 10pm and I was stunned to see hundreds of students coming out of each building filling the entire street at the exact time to go home. Some were getting into the parents' cars waiting in front and some were walking home in groups as there are a lot of apartments nearby because parents consider the area best in terms of providing the best quality education. I shared my surprise with one of my acquaintances who has lived around there for some time and she said that the time when all the students come out used to be 1am in the past, and it's actually an improvement from before in that they now could go home earlier nowadays. In contrast, when I go to my hometown, a mid-sized city in Korea, quite a few people ask me to encourage their kids to have more interest in study because quite a lot of junior high and high school students just don't study or are not interested in studies and some even dropped out. On one side of our society is the over-competition to go to top university while the opposite is filled with students who just give up because they think that there is no hope or no value in even trying because the decks are stacked up against them, while wasting their valuable time and youth on video games, fun and temporary pleasure not ever knowing their unlimited potential within themselves.

In my view, such extremization of motives will never result in a healthy, sound and beautiful society because we all share the same time and space on this earth. None of our lives are perfect but in wherever place we are, we need to go on and not give up while not trying to impose too much restraint and ambition to always be number one. It would be so meaningful if we could live our lives as they are, hoping for the best for the future, doing our best in the current circumstances, never losing the long-term goal that we could be beneficial and exert good influence around us.

# 10. Be Careful with Your Mouth and Heart

## (1) Importance of One Statement

When I attended Thiel College in Greenville, Pennsylvania as an exchange student, we were provided with the opportunities to take private music lessons as part of the program, and I decided to learn the pipe organ because I liked music and I learned to play piano since I was five years old as my dad wanted me to play piano at church. In order to take pipe organ lessons, I had to walk across the main campus to the auditorium, open the backdoor of the stage, turn on the small light by the entrance, walk across the stage and up the narrow stairs to the organ station. The lesson was once a week, but I had to go alone to practice the organ with the dimming light on the corner of stage and organ station, sitting with my back turned against the huge audience seats filled with pitch darkness. I was so scared to go practice whenever I go, and at times, I just came down from the station and left without practicing because the fear of darkness was so overwhelming, and it felt like there was someone sitting in the dark audience seats. However, I liked the sound of the pipe organ and I just could not give up on learning to play it, so I completed two terms of pipe organ lessons with Ms. Florence Jowers with only the sounds of air going through the huge pipes filling the entire ceilings and sides of the stage in such grand darkness.

One day, when we were sitting on the organ, practicing and learning, Ms. Jowers, who was sitting next to me asked, "It's very rare for an exchange student to want to learn pipe organ and I am so impressed that you are learning so fast, even faster than the students who major in pipe organ." And with such complements she suddenly asked what I wanted to do after graduation. I suddenly felt lost because I didn't know what to say and I remember I, for a brief moment, worried if she would be disappointed for me not knowing what I wanted to do. But instantly and to my surprise, I said, "I want to be an international lawyer." I wasn't sure why and how I said it, but there it was, and then she responded even beyond expectation saying that, "I knew that you would do something great because even if you change your major to pipe organ, I am sure you will be a world-renowned organist. I am sure you will be a great lawyer, and now I should go around and show off to people that one of my students would be a great international lawyer!" My response and her reaction were both totally unexpected in that while I knew that deep in my heart I had the small desire that I wanted to be a lawyer for my dad, but it felt so impossible for me to achieve so I never realistically considered it until that time, and she was so complementary and encouraging to almost make me blush. Since then, I sometimes had the silly thought that perhaps I should change my major to pipe organ, based on the professor's excessively kind complement, but even more seriously I started to worry what if I don't become a lawyer now that I told the professor as such, because then I would be dishonest.

After over a decade of working as a lawyer in big law firms in Canada, Singapore and Korea, I now feel that moment was a moment of encouragement that I took in my heart that I could try and be a lawyer. While I had the desire to make my dad proud by becoming a lawyer even if he was living a truly happy and fulfilled life as a pastor because I felt sorry for his daily predicaments as a physically handicapped person and wanted to do something good for him. However, I never verbalized such wishes in my life until that moment maybe because I thought realistically it was an impossible dream or there were too many barriers. But amid the solemn darkness in the huge auditorium under the dim lights of the organ station, I said it unconsciously and abruptly without even thinking and it was indeed the first time in my life that I spoke out about what I wanted to do. If I just superficially answered perhaps I would be a professor or teacher or something else, I probably wouldn't remember that moment, and it would have been impossible to build my life based on one statement made on the spur of the moment like that, but remembering that incident, I believe I could come this far, reaffirming what I said, what I heard and how it was like around us on that day. Therefore, I would like to emphasize that it is essential we at least once verbalize what we want no matter how impossible it seems, but not in a frivolous manner, because once we speak and act more in line with that statement and perhaps we could meet people who could help us move forward towards that direction.

> "The tongue has the power of life and death, and those who love it will eat its fruit." (Proverbs 18:21)

While it feels so light and unimportant, what comes out of our mouth has such an amazing might and influence. Do we say that we mean something, we believe in something, what kind of person we are and what we want? In Korea, there is a saying that, 'A simple word well-spoken can relieve a thousand dollars of debt,' so to speak. One word can lead our lives towards a more positive direction and one word spoken in haste and recklessness could ruin a relationship and damage our prospects. On the other hand, while we need to be always careful with our words, it is also true that it's hard to be always so cautious because I myself make so many blunders with my words. What's most important, in my view, is that we should learn from our mistakes and then resolve to not repeat the missteps and be more careful next time and that should be quite sufficient. Just because we made mistakes or careless statements, we should not feel so discouraged and self-critical and end up with the self-destructive hopelessness, but we should have the courage of heart to stay positive based on the forgiveness and grace of God while, with that encouragement, we step forward and do our best to move forward so that we can push us towards the upward spiral, rather than the downward spiral in our lives.

## (2) Attitude determines altitude

> "Above all else, guard your heart, for everything you do flows from it." (Proverbs 4:23)

In all things we do, truthfully there is nothing more important than attitude more so than background, talents, skills, or inherent ability we are born with. As explained above in relation to the self-fulfilling prophecy, if we think positively, things are more likely to work out positively and vice versa.

> "It is your attitude, more than your aptitude, that will determine your altitude."
>
> – Zig Ziglar

If I did not have the attitude that I would do my best no matter what, I don't think I would have come this far. As a new lawyer at a British law firm in Singapore, one of the daunting tasks was to prepare a syndicated loan agreement that was about 150-200 pages in total based on the term sheet. For one it is very long, and you need to be really meticulous in drafting and reviewing each section carefully coordinating how each section works together to reflect the parties' intent based on the firm's template. Once you start working on it, three of four hours just fly in front of the computer screen because you forget how long it passed being absorbed into the work. If it's not a project financing deal that would probably last more than a couple of years, most standard syndicated financing would close within two or three months and there were more than a couple of transactions concurrently being progressed at any given time. It was a lot of work for the first four or five years as a new lawyer and I worked almost every day past midnight well into the early morning hours. At times I felt like a machine that produces contracts and with the tension in my mind that I should not make mistakes as a professional, I spent the first couple of years entirely focusing on work and absorbed into the repetitive works almost every single day.

Looking back, those time that I did my best to do well in my work while it felt quite boring and unbearable at times built the solid foundation for me to be a good transactional lawyer who knows where certain sections are in the close to 200 or more page-long contracts without even having to look up, how each section work together vis-à-vis the others and which ones are the important negotiation points. Without the humility to learn and do my best during such early years, I don't think I could have endured the seemingly endless period filled with so many difficulties and challenges and likewise in any other areas in lives, our attitude and perspective is so much more important that what talents we have, which school we are from or what we are naturally good at.

## (3) Keep the Balance of Your Heart

We will lose balance in our lives if we are leaning towards one direction, and it is so important to make consistent and intentional efforts to maintain that balance. Moreover, even when we at times lose our balance and make regrettable missteps, we should stay positive to not lose heart.

For instance, humility is one. Sometimes I think my mom lacks balanced self-esteem when I see her overly considerate of others and not respecting herself. But when I see her always believing the best in others, covering and forgiving their transgressions and impoliteness, and generously giving with unbelievable compassion and kindness, I sense the real manifestation of God's love towards us, and I feel that I should be more generous in resemblance of God and the example of my mom. In contrast, a person without self-esteem on the other extreme is a person who is arrogant and full of him or herself that nobody truly likes. Of course, we could lose our balance and act arrogantly at times, but still we need to have the courage of heart to not give up and do better, after true repentance and reflection.

Nobody is perfect, and balance is important because it is so easy to lose it. In a way it is more important to keep getting it back, rather than always trying to maintain it considering how each moment we tend to lose it with so many distractions and temptations.

Other examples are criticism and nonchalance. If too critical, we continuously complain and are always skeptical of others. There are always good reasons to be critical, but we need to maintain a good balance and discernment between criticism and blind endorsement or indifference.

**Serenity Prayer**
God, grant me the serenity to accept the things I cannot change,
Courage to change the things I can, and wisdom to know the difference.

The same goes for the thought and action. While I highlighted the importance of thinking carefully about the implication of our action whether it would lead to an upward or downward spiral, too much thinking without action would not make a difference at all. In contrast, people who hastily act without thinking carefully will end up regretting their actions on many occasions. We should keep the ideal balance between the thought and action and act wisely.

## (4) Stay Patient for the Positive Turning Point

Our lives are in the hands of God in that no matter how hopeless it seems, He will deliver us and lead us to the right path. That does not mean that we don't do anything and just pray and wait for Him to do something, wasting our lives or indulging in the self-destructive thoughts, habits and behaviors. Doing our best given the circumstances and staying positive will result in an amazing outcome that we could not have foreseen or imagined before. While things move so slowly, and it appears that nothing is happening, over time we may witness a huge accomplishment in the end if we keep on keeping on. That principle is frequently called as the "Law of Gradual Progress", which can be viewed in two opposite ways. One is that we really need to do our best and not give up on small tasks each day no matter how it seems insignificant and trivial compared with our grand vision and purpose in life. The other is that even when you can't see the future with any vision and there seems no hope due to the severity of current misery, we still focus on what's the best course of action at this moment and doing our best with humble and sincere attitude will somehow lead us to an amazing and unbelievable achievement over time.

I worked very hard since I became a lawyer recording high billable hours for many years but once I gave birth to my second child in October 2015, I started to have huge conflict as to whether I should give up on working for a big law firm because I could no longer prioritize my work as I have done in the past. In general, big law firms require the absolute commitment prioritizing work over personal lives and I remember one of the articling students shared the secret '10 minute rule' (or was it three) for success that we should respond to senior lawyer's request for work or assignment within 10 minutes or we are basically out. Anyways, I truly enjoyed work and responsibility as my personality fits in that I take responsibility for the work that's given to me wholeheartedly, and I could go on working fully-committed until I had my second child. Around mid-2016, I seriously started thinking about taking a couple of years off from work to prioritize childcare and as I really didn't want to give up on work despite the inevitable need at home, I had a lot on my mind and could not decide.

In one of those days, out of nowhere, an existing client based in Europe requested a fee quote whether we could assist with a complicated securitization transaction around June. It was not my area of expertise as I focus more on loans but thankfully there was an expert in that area in our team who moved over to Yulchon a few months ago, so he and I decided to work on that transaction as a team with other associates and we confirmed as such with the client by end of June. But then, suddenly my sister died at the end of July and I was under unbelievable shock, anguish and sorrow through the experience and felt tempted to take a break immediately.

However, while I could hand over all the other works and assignments to other colleagues, that securitization transaction somehow made me feel that I should be responsible no matter how hard it was for me, and such obligatory feeling was hard to explain but it felt like it was a personal promise with the client that I made that I would be responsible to close successfully because the client gave our team the trust to complete the work even if our team never worked on it before. So, while it was hard to concentrate on work and there was strong temptation to give up, I decided not to give up and did my best to focus on work and successfully closed that transaction working efficiently with arrangers and other related and counterparties and their counsels by the requested timeline. After the successful closing at the end of October, I discussed with the senior members of the firm that I wanted to go on an extended leave in November, and I took that leave away from work from December 2016 thanks to the consideration of the senior members of the firm.

This chain of events may seem insignificant, but I fully appreciate how accurate God is by the minute in orchestrating our lives. If the client approached us after my sister died, probably I would have handed that work over to a colleague as I did not have the strength in my heart to go on at that stage. However, the client requested our assistance just before my sister's death and I already committed to the work. Also, there was an excellent expert in that area who joined our team from another big firm a few months ago who could lead the transaction, and he was supportive in working with me as he appreciated what I was going through and we worked as a team very well and the client was very appreciative of our hard work and efficient management of the transaction to the successful closing.

Furthermore, in early August one of the senior executives of a major conglomerate in Korea urgently requested our help for a matter that needed to be resolved in two or three days, and I coordinated with the senior members who have the capacity to resolve the issue immediately and we could achieve a positive outcome working efficiently and following up diligently. Mainly through these memorable works in the mourning period soon after my sister's death, I could get out of bed that I just wanted to stay in the morning, continued to care for my two little ones and did my best with the work as a lawyer in the most challenging times of my life.

Of course a thought came to my mind when that senior executive contacted me that I could just say to him that, "I am really sorry but something happened to me recently and unfortunately I can't help you with this," and perhaps I could have asked one of my colleagues to help out instead of myself, and even if I said that he and anyone else would probably say it was natural that I refused to help and let someone else help instead as what I was going through was a lot. However, I consciously chose to help when I was in agony, and because of that choice, I could restore my strength also to carry on with my life and stay focused on what needed to be done each day while going through the painful mourning period, instead of being absorbed into the dark pit of sadness and misery. Through these experiences, I realized what it means to make a positive choice even if you are in difficult and challenging circumstances and how important that is.

It is indeed hard to consciously think about the weight of each decision and choice we make in that it would lead us to a certain direction because we are so busy each day each moment. However, if we reflect on our choices and their tendencies and characteristics, we can appreciate how even a seemingly trivial choice is in fact quite significant in shaping our lives. In particular, when we need to make a decision once something bad or unexpected happened, we definitely need to think carefully about what choices we are making in connection therewith. No matter how tempting it is to just soak in our deep despair and misery, nursing on our injury and not doing anything, let us have the courage to step out to help others and do some meaningful work notwithstanding the hurt, pain, sadness, disappointment and despair. In so doing, we will one day realize that our pain and suffering has gradually resolved, and we are restored while there are also a lot of unexpected constructive ramifications of our good-willed endeavors helping others as well as ourselves.

I am pretty sure that if I did not focus on the works that needed to be done after my sister's death, I would probably have had some form of depression being absorbed into the pain of the sudden loss. It still hurts me, and I am in tears even now thinking about my beautiful and kind-hearted sister and her permanent absence from this world, but I believe I endured the hardest mourning period of all thanks to God's providence and my faithful, albeit how unwilling I was or how impossible it seemed, obedience to His plan, and I do my best to stay grateful to God's mysterious workings in timing and His love and plan for our lives. So, every single day, I open my eyes and resolve each morning that I will live to the best I can relying on Him, and I share my dad's "Five Meditation Prayer", which he created and made into a hymn a few years ago.

### Five Meditation Prayer – Yong-Heon Sohn, Pastor

1. God is the Holy Spirit and the God of Salvation who is self-existing in twelve inherent characters. He created the universe with His words and still works to fulfill His plan to save us and will judge the universe at the end of history according to the bible.

2. Jesus is the Holy Son and Savior, who came to earth to save us and bear the cross. He resurrected after death and went to heaven to later return to bring us home. He says we should live in hope of His coming back and in heavenly joy even on this earth.

3. Holy Spirit is the third trinity, who graciously helps us and is responsible for our salvation and the Comforter who revives the dead spirit in us and teaches and helps us to remember God's words. He graciously fulfills our salvation each day.

4. I am a person who was created in His image, who inherited the sins of Adam. I didn't know God but became the child of God through His grace and love, and I can secure the heaven in His love. I will live my life with God from now until eternity.

5. I shall live, being thankful and obedient, remembering His grace and pursuant to His plan. Truly repenting my wrongdoings and changing my ways, I will fulfill my calling and be more like Jesus. I begin today, humbly entrusting my whole life with my Lord.

My dad made this song and gave the homework (!) to all church members to memorize it, and every morning service is finished with the recital of this hymn altogether. I am quite inspired by this song, thinking about how it encapsulates all the essential points of Christianity and how limited his access to information is in this age of smartphones and internet for I know how he has very minimal recourse to widely available sermons, helpful materials and other related resources richly available for those other pastors with eyesight. I am encouraged in my faith by singing this hymn whenever I am confused and at the verge of losing my faith in the face of unbelievable forces of darkness that seems to dominate the universe and causes so many unfortunate and disastrous happenings in our lives.

As I have shared in my experience above, there will be a positive turning point in our life as long as we hold onto our faith in God and His plan for our lives no matter how negative it seems and those turning point tends to happen quite unexpectedly. There is an expression, "God works in mysterious ways." Those who experienced His miracles in such an unexpected manner would appreciate what this means. For example, those who we believed that would help may turn their back against us when we are vulnerable, but some strangers may accidently help us. Our simple unintentional kind word may save a person's life that day.

I wish all of us could live our lives richly experiencing such mysterious helping hands of God as often as possible. And I wish none of us give up prematurely before we experience such miracles just because we could not get over our lopsided negative thinking focusing on the downsides, challenges and impediments in our lives, being absorbed in our hopelessness and desolation indulging in the self-destructive and self-sabotaging habits and behaviors. And until that positive turning point appears, I hope we can ceaselessly make positive choices each moment and each day, faithfully believing Him and His words encouraging us every day to live joyfully no matter how challenging and impenetrable the obstacles may be.

## (5) Never Lose Your Smile

I want to introduce Ingrid Betancourt, senator and presidential candidate in Columbia back in early 2000. She was born on

December 25, 1961, but in the course of campaigning for presidency, she was kidnapped by the Revolutionary Army Forces of Columbia in February 2002 and held captive in forest camp until July 2008 when she was unexpectedly rescued. She is so beautiful and feminine, and it is hard to imagine the hardship of being under captivity for over six years, and her survival truly manifests the unlimited potential of human mind and strong will.

> "I knew of no instruction manual for reaching a higher level of humanity and a greater wisdom. But I felt intuitively that laughter was the beginning of wisdom, as it was indispensable for survival."
>
> – Ingrid Betancourt

A smile is the global language that everybody can speak, and especially the language of God because I am sure that He is smiling at us with indescribable love and grace as we are the children of His. We know how we can't stop smiling whenever we see our kids, and so we should also know how He feels toward us. Like our Father, we should never lose our smile and be positive no matter what difficulties we may face and always hold onto the affirmative power of smile that comes to our heart instantly at the moment we try.

## (6) Keep Working on Thinking Positively

True positive thinking doesn't mean the denial or absence of difficulty or challenges in our lives; rather, it is proactively acknowledging and embracing such dark force in our lives, and still move forward with small and big choices in an optimistic and constructive manner in reliance of a persistent faith in God. Such positive thinking means giving time for ourselves to mourn and reflect on our lives, ourselves, people around us, and most importantly His love and grace towards our lives when we are faced with unexpected tribulations. Once a glass or mirror is broken, the pieces seem useless and dangerous, but from the eyes of the thoughtful artist, each piece may be seen as the meaningful instrument to complete a masterpiece. In my view, true positivity can never be light or frivolous as in temporary pleasure or enjoyment relying on alcohol, drugs, entertainment or other forms of indulgences. While we may benefit from such temporary escape at times, we should know deep in our heart that the only genuine positivity comes from the One who created this universe and each of our existence and wants to save us from the force of darkness and make us as His own.

Moreover, true faith in the Almighty God will not allow us to stay doomed, distressed, distrustful, selfish or separated from other people in our little room, and will always push us to rise up and shine His light that is in us and share His love and grace with as many people as possible as the light shines through the deepest darkness in this world. Even in the midst of a deep sense of loss and pain in our heart, if we have that boundless source of positivity that is from God, we have the capacity to infinitely love and encourage ourselves and others even if our eyes are still filled with tears and our heart is throbbing in pain. Hence, the broken glasses can be transformed into an amazing glass art piece inspiring many people with the stunning beauty and the capacity to overcome the pain and damage that was inflicted in the past. As Senator Kennedy said, we should get over our obsession with perfection, embrace our imperfection and missteps, and endeavor to make the small changes that are possible and do our best to continue to make affirmative choices toward an upward spiral of our lives.

# 11.
# Of Course, Work Hard

### (1) True Effort means Commitment

Malcolm Gladwell, in his book entitled, "Outliers: The Story of Success," introduced the law of 10,000 hours. Successful people, no matter how ingenious he or she may be, still invested 10,000 hours into the area that they are good at in order to excel. His theory is quite convincing and illuminating. Whenever my dad heads his way to church with the heavy machine that reads the bible for the blind on his shoulder (and that side is always slanted down for the weight), I think of the image of 'commitment'.

One of my uncles who helped at the beginning of my dad's church said, he was so inspired by my dad's kneeling down and reading the braille bible every second that he got in between the acupuncture sessions. Before my dad committed to the full-time ministry, he was a professional acupuncturist, and in a room filled with patients, he dedicated every small break in between sessions reading bible and praying, and with that sort of commitment he has become the pastor that he is now with such firm conviction and fundamental depth of knowledge and inspiration.

> "The irony of commitment is that it's deeply liberating – in work, in play, in love. The act frees you from the tyranny of your internal critic, from the fear that likes to dress itself up and parade around as rational hesitation. To commit is to remove your head as the barrier to your life."
>
> – Anne Morris

If we tend to think too much, hesitate, or are full of fear and doubt, we should focus on working on commitment. Once we have made a decision on one thing after a long debate in our minds, then we should commit ourselves without any further doubt or regret.

Also let us be aware that there is no one on this earth who doesn't have emotional barriers like fear or doubt, and we should not be so naïve to fall into the trap of the devil who lies that we are the only ones who continue to make missteps, who continue to feel threatened, fearful and unclear. Notwithstanding the apparent presence of all those negative emotions in our lives, we can still make a small positive choice each moment and each day toward the direction of an upward spiral of our lives.

## (2) Study Efficiently

My father emphasizes the importance of the saying 'Think from the Other's Perspective' and gave a plaque inscribed with this message to me and my siblings as his 60$^{th}$ birthday celebration gift. While he emphasized this approach for ideal spousal relationship wishing that he wanted us to live peacefully and happily amongst family members, this mental approach is quite efficient and valuable in most of other human relationships as well.

Owners should think how they can make employees feel valued and motivated to work hard whereas employees should think about how the owners would want the ideal employees should be. Husbands should think about what types of husbands the wives would want and vice versa. The same applies to the friends, colleagues, neighbors and many other relationships.

When we study as well, it is important to remember what the tester, teacher or author wants to teach us, and focus on the main points before just approaching without any specific framework in our minds. It is important to learn, read and study in an efficient manner.

### (3) Manage Your Energy

Life is very short, and we live only once. We organize our lives based on the 24-hour day and we may at times feel that the daily routine is just so boring, and it is just an endless repetition. In contrast, we may suddenly have an unpredicted, disastrous accident and we are embroiled in an emotional storm. Whenever I am in the middle of emotional turmoil due to internal or external threats or uncontrollable factors, I am reminded of efficient energy management, which suggests that emotion is also type of energy in that our various feelings including sorrow, loneliness, regret and resentment are all forms of energy that sustains our body, and they are not unlimited and need to be managed efficiently.

Therefore, when we are faced with a deep sense of loss, it is necessary to go through the mourning period, but let us set a period to feel sad at some point and divert our attention to something else that could help us such as good music, praises, songs, movies, bible, good books, good friends, family and close relatives. By thinking that we need energy management and emotion is also part of energy that need to be understood well, utilized and managed well help us to cope better when an unforeseen accident or something daunting happens in our lives.

### (4) Over-delivery

When I study or work, I always think about how I can overdeliver in terms of quality of the deliverables and whether I could add value in any way. I think from the client's perspective when requested to undertake certain legal work or major tasks and always tried to overdeliver to the extent possible. Therefore, I have often heard clients and seniors expressing gratitude and complements that my work results are quite different from others in that it really looks as if I paid more attention to it and I took ownership of the work product as if it was my own work in such a sincere manner.

If we do the work just to make money or out of obligation, there is a higher risk of oversights or errors. Even those who are objectively smart people tend to make mistakes at work sometimes, because they don't have that mindset to own the work as if it is their own and take responsibility to do it better. So, I am in some way proud to say that it has been almost non-existent that I made any major mistakes in managing a project or completing a transaction to date because I always approach work as if I must be 100% responsible all the time and I always double check the documents and deliverables a couple of times to ensure quality.

It's a huge commitment and the sense of priority should be there; however, this attitude may frustrate some other people because I have this bad habit of checking twice or three times in my daily routine as well at times, so I am fully aware that finding the healthy balance and having humility that my strengths can be my weakness at the same time is so important.

# 12. Respect and Encourage Each Other

### (1) We All Need a Village

In 1996, Hillary Rodham Clinton wrote the book entitled, "It Takes a Village; and Other Lessons Children Teach Us", highlighting the importance of 'shared responsibility' to bring up children because to bring up a child efficiently it's not just the family who is accountable but rather it's the other parts of society including village, society and community who should share this important responsibility. Those who should play important roles are direct family members, grandparents, neighbors, teachers, pastors, doctors, employers, politicians, NGOs, churches, other religious organizations, corporations and international institutions.

The need for a village can be viewed from various perspectives. All of us now remember we used to be children once who looked up to adults, and we still have aspect of childlikeness in all of us until the moment we die. In fact, all of us truthfully need a village considering that there is no one single person in this world who is so perfect and who can live in isolation from other people. No matter how great somebody is, he or she would have inevitable vulnerability or weakness as a human being. On the other hand, even if a person is physically disabled, he or she may have a much deeper character and honorable mindset and lifestyle than a physically able person; hence, is able to play a significant role in the community. That's why we need to embrace and encourage each other and there should also be systematic support structure to ensure our children grow up in the most desirable and supportive environment possible. Even for our own wellbeing and happiness as well, it is so important that we make our place a beautiful village to support each other in a positive way rather than just focusing on our individual pleasure or isolated enjoyment.

Regarding this argument that we need a village, I find two regrettable issues relating to Sarah, my sister. Perhaps I didn't know her that well because we lived separately since university years as I lived away in Seoul but anyways, there are two observations that I want to share. First, a lot of children in our society are not so blessed with perfect parents and the most ideal nurturing home environment, so that's why we need other parts of overall social structure to work seamlessly to support our children in various aspects. As mentioned in several places, my parents are very dedicated, conservative and old-fashioned pastor and wife, strictly abiding by the biblical principles and combined with my dad's handicap, they could not devote much time on their kids' education like other overly-zealous parents with high ambition and drive for secular success.

My parents were always busy with church affairs, my dad preparing sermons more than 15 times a week including morning services based on limited resources because he didn't have access to many reading materials available on internet or bookstores, and my parents were always attending to some matters of church members, their sickness and other various visitations. Also, as mentioned earlier, my parents never mentioned the importance of success or excellence at school, but highlighted the importance of faith and obedience to God. So, in a sense, study was only ancillary priority to being a good Christian.

In such conservative and in some way restrictive environment always under the burden of having to act well and be the ideal Christian as pastor's kids, Sarah started thinking that she was not loved and did not fit into our family since young. I was immature in that instead of comforting her and being a good sister, I looked down on her for not doing well at school and not listening to our parents. She was so beautiful, brave, kind, talented at arts and drawing, excellent at cooking and licensed as nutritionist after majoring in food and nutrition in university. But her life was cut short so sadly and why... In essence, we failed at providing the best environment for her, and the schools and all the other institutions were not perfect either in various ways.

Taking one step further and apart from our case, we are fully aware that so many children in the world are exposed to undesirable, damaging environment, abuse and mistreatment and there are so many incomprehensible injustices done to such young and helpless kids. There is no perfect home, family, school, teacher or institution, but all of us should endeavor to work in concert to build an ideal community for our children because we all live in harmony rather than separated as islands. If someone is thinking incorrectly and leading his or her life down the wrong path, there should be multiple layers of support readily available and organically working together in society to bring that person back to the right path to find meaning and joy in life, fulfilling the role of the constructive member of the community.

Second, while it is so heartbreaking to acknowledge it, I want to highlight the obvious presence of evil forces and their influence and, furthermore, how we should all endeavor to have positive influence and work together to fight against such force of darkness in our society. Sarah did not have a lot of good friends, and unfortunately at times considered our parents' concerns as nagging and didn't want to listen. Sadly, I became aware of one incident which probably exacerbated her insomnia. A few years ago, she happened to live alone next to her friend and her mother's one-room apartment, and hers was recently renovated and looked really nice. Apparently, her friend and her mother visited Sarah's place one day, and they were so impressed to the extent that they wanted to move in somehow. So, her friend's mother, who happened to be a fortuneteller and shaman or something, told Sarah that there was a ghost in her unit. It is just so dumbfounding how ill-intentioned and greedy her friend's mother was that she breathed in such fear in Sarah, clearly knowing that she was living alone and vulnerable.

Since then, I heard that her fear of darkness worsened and could not sleep well at night. Her friend was not the true friend who would help in times of need, and her friend's mother is true force of evil who harms others for her own greed, desires and selfishness. The bible clearly states that the devil came to steal, kill and destroy while Jesus came to give us life to the full. Those who are used by the devil and those who exert evil influences are clearly present in our society.

In the common law system, there is a movement for restorative justice to have more compassion for the criminals because they themselves were most likely the victims of childhood abuse or other forms of violence or crimes. However, such an approach would fall on deaf ears on the family members of the victims who suffer from the enormous sense of loss. Furthermore, even if we were a victim of childhood abuse or any other type of unfortunate incident, environment and mistreatment, it is of course so upsetting and deeply hurtful, but we now have the power to choose what kind of person we want to become, instead of staying at the level of equally wanting to hurt others because we were hurt in the past. We as Christians who are forgiven, saved and given a second chance in life as a new creation, we inevitably become profoundly grateful, compassionate, generous and forgiving, and we also realize that we have the freedom to resolve that we want to live as the light and be the force of positivity toward the upward spiral no matter what happened in the past that was beyond our control.

I hope that we use our authentic power to choose wisely and constructively, and there are more and more optimistic and uplifting people in this world so that we make the place we live better and for that we should spread the Good News, which enables ultimate transformation in ourselves no matter how damaged or wounded we are and how impossible or hopeless it seems.

As introduced earlier, Malcolm Gladwell highlighted the importance of community and common values in his book, Outliers. Nobody grew up independently and we all were loved and taken care of when we were mere infants. We all need others who could pay attention to us and comfort us when we go through difficult, confusing times and upsetting moments in our lives. I am so disheartened to see young students leaving home in defiance of their parents or caretakers because they hated their elders' nagging or interference and end up with evil people who take advantage of them for their own greed and bodily desires.

Against such evil force, people with good and decent hearts should work together fiercely to make our place better for our sake and for the sake of our young ones. In my view, those young ones who leave their family at such an early age to do it on their own tend to be good-hearted but ill-directed. They are probably born into a poor or disadvantageous family environment, and because they don't want to be a burden to the family, they decide to do it on their own based on their misguided thinking, and yet unfortunately most of them end up getting into the hands of evil people who exploit them. So that's why it is so important that we need to help our young ones think right and not be absorbed into their wrong thinking and make a huge misstep in their lives, erroneously and unconsciously leading toward a self-destructive direction.

I once talked in front of a few junior high and high school students on the subject of, 'Why we need to study'. Preparing that talk, I remembered how I also hated studying at some point because it felt so boring, useless and endless. In particular, there are so many fun things that are tempting our kids instead of studies, such as video games, TV and internet. However, if we just look a little further, we know that in some countries child labor is prevalent in that even five-year olds are pulled into labor market, having to make money to support the family and sustain a livelihood. As to why we need to study, I highlighted that the mandatory primary, junior high and high schools are precious 'present' for young ones as it is indeed a gift, invaluable 'opportunity' and important 'preparation' for our future no matter how frustrating and boring it seems, presenting the data on child labor where such gift, opportunity and preparation is not provided or guaranteed.

We all need to start making money or play a certain role in society once we graduate from high school or university, and we can utilize the education system to reflect on and prepare and decide on what type of role we want to play in society. Therefore, if our kids appreciate the mandatory school system as a special gift, valuable opportunity and crucial preparation for the rest of their lives, I believe they would study harder voluntarily and sincerely. If not, it is probably because we adults are not doing the job of helping them realize as such.

Unfortunately, there is no perfect educational system that prepares our children in most ideal way because in our life nothing is in fact ultimately perfect, but we all should do our best to the extent possible. Furthermore, what I want to emphasize is that if the school system is not perfect, if the individual household is not most ideal, and kids are disoriented and tend to drop out, then we should have other entities in society, supplementing and complementing each other to ensure there are layers of well-intentioned and trustworthy institutions that endeavor to support our solid societal structure and provide a safe and encouraging environment for our kids. In this regard, I hope we pay more attention to other people as well, in addition to ourselves, our families and our own kids, with the gracious and warm heart towards many people out there who may benefit from our kindness and therefore end up making our place ultimately better, healthier and greater.

### (2) Mutual Respect

Studying at Thiel College as an exchange student was my first study abroad experience, and of course I thought I would continue with my graduate studies in the US like most Koreans do, but I happened to marry a Korean-Canadian who was so trustworthy and loving and that's how I became familiar with

Canada, decided to study in Canada and ended up becoming a Canadian lawyer. While it is all relative, what stands out regarding Canada and its culture is that it's quite different from Korea in terms of looking at the job hierarchy in that there is less prestige or shame associated with certain categories of jobs. In Korea, there is a strong preference to have highly educated elite jobs in comparison to physical labor or more menial work which drives overly-competitive environment at schools as well as in society, but to a certain degree, in Canada people seem to consider all job categories on relatively equal footings in that it's just work that you do and then there is your personal life with family that you have to go back that is more important and meaningful. In some way, the overall sentiment is that everybody's labor is respected, and it doesn't mean that someone's job is better than others' just because it's more prestigious, highly educated or better paid.

Malcolm Gladwell introduces the city of Roseto in his book, Outliers where he explains the mysteriously healthy community in such an intriguing manner. Roseto is a small town of about 2,000 people composed of immigrants from the same city in Italy, which formed the entire city around the church called Our Lady of Mount Carmine in the middle, and there are vibrant commercial and farming activities organically organized and expanded encompassing the entire community. Quizzically, one doctor accidentally noticed a unique feature of this city around 1950s that there was extremely low rate of heart attack (more than 50% lower than other cities amongst over 65 seniors' heart attack and there was none who died from heart attack below 55 years old in Roseto) in comparison with other similar cities. In addition, overall death rate was 30-35% lower than other cities, and there was no suicide, no alcoholics, no drug addicts and extremely low crime rates and no extremely poor people in that city. With these unique findings, quite a few medical doctors and scholars decided to study this city to figure out the reasons behind such outstanding features, and they found that there was no other conclusion than that it was only because it was Roseto itself. Roseto was a real community where everybody genuinely shared a common value proposition that Rosetans cherished their community and supported each other in such an organic, caring and compassionate manner.

> "What Wolf began to realize was that the secret of Roseto wasn't diet or exercise or genes or location. It had to be Roseto itself. As Bruhn and Wolf walked around the town, they figured out why. They looked at how the Rosetans visited one another, stopping to chat in Italian on the street,

say, or cooking for one another in their backyards. They learned about the extended family clans that underlay the town's social structure. They saw how many homes had three generations living under one roof, and how much respect grandparents commanded. They went to mass at Our Lady of Mount Carmel and saw the unifying and calming effect of the church. They counted twenty-two separate civic organizations in a town of just under two thousand people. They picked up on the particular egalitarian ethos of the community, which discouraged the wealthy from flaunting their success and helped the unsuccessful obscure their failures... Living a long life, the conventional wisdom at the time said, depended to a great extent on who we were – that is, our genes. It depended on the decisions we made – on what we chose to eat, and how much we chose to exercise, and how effectively we were treated by the medical system. No one was used to thinking about health in terms of "community". Wolf and Bruhn had to convince the medical establishment to think about health and heart attacks in an entirely new way: They had to get them to realize that they wouldn't be able to understand why someone was healthy if all they did was think about an individual's personal choices or actions in isolation. They had to look "beyond" the individual. They had to understand the culture he or she was a part of, and who their friends and families were, and what town their families came from. They had to appreciate the idea that the values of the world we inhabit and the people we surround ourselves with have a profound effect on who we are." (Pages 9-11, Outliers: The Story of Success)

As long as our happiness is defined by what schools we go to, what job we will have, and how much money we will make, with the fixed viewpoint that certain jobs are absolutely preferable and honorable while others are looked down, we lose healthy balance in our perspectives and in life, and end up living miserably, constantly competing to get ahead and be better than others, enslaved by our uneven thoughts and prejudice. In the end, we are living together sharing one earth, one time in long history, needing each other's help and respective roles in the shared place and time, called 'here' and 'now'. A genuine community with love, care and respect for each other provides the opportunity for us to live a much better life than overly-competitive, non-caring and self-absorbed lifestyle in the long run.

## (3) Mutual Encouragement

While we may be successful, perfect and alright at this moment, we have no idea what lies ahead and there is no way we can avoid our ultimate demise at the end of our lives whenever that may be. Not even the smartest person knows when their life will end, but ironically, we live under the misguided belief that we are the smartest who knows it all. A sudden incident can change our lives instantly, and there are so many possibilities in our lives that may lead our lives toward a better or worse direction.

Even when we have been leaning toward a negative direction, we may suddenly make a detour and turn toward an unbelievably positive direction, thanks to somebody's one kind word of encouragement or some desirable influence of strangers. Or we may waste our lives not even knowing the unlimited potential of our lives because of the bad influence or undesirable environment, as we have seen in the case of the eagle who believed that it was a chicken. That's why it is so important to look around and try to help others to see if any of us are suffering from any erroneous thinking, unfortunate difficulties, or if any of us need encouragement today and whether there is anything we could do to support others to live better, rather than living a life focusing only on ourselves.

In connection with my humble observation on the overly-competitive social environment in Korea, I sincerely hope that we all have more caring heart for each other, rather than just to excel and get ahead to live a successful life as highlighted above sharing the example of Roseto. In addition, I deeply hope that we could have a kind and generous attitude toward the weak, the vulnerable, the underprivileged and the handicapped. In this regard, I want to share three main experiences while studying outside of Korea.

First, I studied as an exchange student in US as stated above and one of the notable characteristics of Americans and Canadians particularly in small cities like Greenville, Pennsylvania that I studied is that people smile a lot. Even when you don't know the other person, if your eyes are crossed, you just smile and ask, "Hi, how are you or good morning" and all. For whatever reason, I unconsciously picked up that habit of smiling at strangers, and I tend to smile a lot for no reason even to this date. At that time, one of the professors at Thiel College suggested that perhaps my English name should be Sunny because I have such a bright smile like the sun. So, I started using Sunny as my English name for the time being as I didn't have an official English name, but later when I worked in Singapore, one of the other colleagues was already Sunny, so I gave in and instead started using Esther, which is the Christian name that my parents call me at home.

Some people in Korea when I returned to Korea after more than a decade of living overseas criticized me at times that I smile too often. Sometimes it is correct that I smile unnecessarily because even when I feel sorry, I unconsciously make a facial expression that looks like a smile perhaps for purposes of easing the awkwardness or express my regret in a more amicable manner. However, the other person may take such smile or my unconscious effort in a negative or sarcastic way, which is fully understandable. So, I acknowledge that my habit of frequent smile is both my merit and demerit.

However, ultimately, I believe the capacity to smile in the face of challenges and difficulties in our daily lives is an expression of our willfulness to approach the situation in the most affirmative and constructive way possible. Of course, it is impossible to imagine greeting strangers with smile for no reason in the busy streets of

Seoul, and I am fully aware that such culture of smile is also hard to find in big cities like New York or Toronto. But let us sometimes think about the importance of small gesture like smile in our daily lives, as we all need encouragement through our lives no matter how trivial it looks from time to time.

Second, what stands out in my experiences of living abroad is the accommodation and support for the weak. When I was attending the law school, I took a bus one day and was quite shocked. The bus was quite crowded at that time but at one stop, the bus made a full stop lowering the front entrance to enable the wheelchaired passenger to get on, and it took quite some time for that passenger to alight and wear the seatbelt around the wheelchair in the bus.

What surprised me was nobody including the driver or many passengers complained that it took such a long time. Everybody was waiting quietly until that wheelchaired passenger sat securely and instead of complaining, most of the passengers actually looked at the wheelchaired passenger with caring eyes to see if he needed any help. Such scene is hard to imagine in busy Seoul life. We are so incredibly busy and hurried almost all the time. In fact, some people, including myself regrettably, may consider the time that needed to be spent for that one passenger sacrificing many other passengers' time is not economically efficient. However, that experience somehow keeps coming back to my mind occasionally, making me think about what efficiency is, what is meaningful and what is most important in our lives.

What seems clear to me is that the true attractiveness of the strong is not that he or she has all the power and might on this earth to win in any war or fight, but rather that he or she has the immeasurably big heart to sympathize, help and accommodate the weak. The allure of the rich is not because he or she is capable of enjoying all the wealth of this world for his or her pleasure, but rather because he or she is generous and kind enough to share the wealth with those who are in need.

At times no matter how inefficient it seems, if we take the time and efforts to accommodate the underprivileged, the vulnerable and the handicapped and if there are more people who are compassionate and considerate with profoundly generous and kind heart, I firmly believe that we can move toward a more enriching and formidable community where the majority of people can lead a happy and mutually beneficial lives and share in the common goods that our society has to offer and minimize the structural problems such as extremization of motives, poverty, class conflicts, suicide or other prevalent crimes in our society.

Last but not least, I want to highlight the difference in the fundamental view toward the handicapped in our society. When I was attending the law school, my parents visited me in Vancouver and I noticed how people reacted when they noticed that my father was blind. Initially some people smile at strangers, but once they noticed that my dad was blind, they showed further interest and made sure they smile one more time, and some people even came up to us and asked what happened and complimented that my dad had such a good smile despite the physical hardship. That experience was such a contrast to what I remember growing up in Korea. At times, people did not hesitate to show contempt or despise toward the handicap on the street or at restaurants and other public places as physical handicap was considered as something unlucky in Korea back in 1980s in my recollection. I assume it was worse in the previous years. In Canada, I was able to feel the warmth, compassion, humanism and kind consideration from the strangers' gaze and glances.

It's just so minor and trivial but I believe that, 'the devil is indeed in the details'. Our beliefs and attitude show in the smallest reaction to different types of people in our society. Each of us no matter how great achievement we have attained would not be considered as great individuals or success without the heart to be sympathetic or pay attention to and take care of the weak and the vulnerable in our society. Zig Ziglar highlights the importance of encouragement as follows:

> "You never know when one kind act or word of encouragement can change a life forever."

In closing, I want to introduce the quote of Ingrid Betancourt, a politician in Columbia who was kidnapped during her presidential campaign by the rebel who was held captive in the forest for six and a half years before the sudden release.

> "You can start right now. Nothing should ever upset you…
> In this condition of the most devastating humiliation, I still possessed the most precious of liberties, that no-one could take away from me: that of deciding who I wanted to be."

As stated earlier, unexpected difficulties and hardships can happen to us at any given time, and we all are subject to the indescribable pain, tremendous heartache and deep sorrow as a result. I believe no single person in this world can claim that he or she is free from any of the common human suffering and negative emotions like disappointment, loneliness, fear, doubt or resentment at some point. We all suffer from regret, failure, mistakes, shame and guilt over what happened or what we did. That is why it is so critical that we encourage each other and endeavor to establish a supportive system like a genuine village where people actually care for each other in our society.

And the most powerful force to enable the true courage to live one's life to the full and share warm encouragement to each other is not the various self-help mechanisms or psychological frameworks of positive mindset or miserable self-deliverance, but rather the belief in God who loves us unconditionally, has special plans for each of us and has given particular environment, unique character, merits, strengths and life events to each of us and is even at this very moment looking at us with a big and warm smile despite our ongoing blunders and inadequacies.

So, let us use our authentic power to choose wisely and carefully, choosing God no matter what so that we experience the true resilience toward the positive upward spiral while concurrently encouraging each other to achieve unbelievable synergy in our community. Let us not give up resorting to our own prejudices, flawed or misguided thoughts, self-destructive habits or rigid viewpoints that refuse to see any hope in a given situation because of the overwhelming weight of the crisis, hardship, pain, disappointment, hurt, regret, sense of loss and confusion and respond by taking the seemingly natural decision towards a downward spiral. Let us go beyond just trying to do it all our own, giving up and letting go if it does not work out. And let us take the courage to ask for help and especially rely on God to stand firmly on His promises, to endure, to not give up, to go on and carry on and to shine our small light in this dark world by voicing our small but powerful affirmative voice to encourage and help each other to head toward the immeasurably beautiful and formidable upward spiral together.

Author
Esther Eun-Jeong (EJ) Sohn

Esther Eun-Jeong Sohn is a senior foreign attorney at Yulchon LLC and her practice focuses on finance and general corporate transactions. Before joining Yulchon, Ms. Sohn worked as an associate for more than 5 years at Lovells Lee & Lee, Watson, Farley & Williams and Holman Fenwick Willan in their Singapore offices after having articled at Stikeman Elliott in Toronto, Canada. Ms. Sohn has represented a variety of clients, including a syndicate of senior lenders, security agents/trustees, mandated lead arrangers, equity investors, borrowers, lessees and project companies, in connection with a range of general corporate commercial and financing transactions, including project finance, syndicated or structured financing, acquisition finance, ship finance, debt restructuring/re-financing, lease transactions and M&As.

Ms. Sohn received her LL.B. from the University of British Columbia in 2005 and received the Bull Housser & Tupper Academic Awards in Technology Law and the Jongman Kim Memorial Academic Awards in Korean Legal Studies. She obtained her M.A. in Sociology in Education from the University of Toronto and graduated Magna Cum Laude from Ewha Womans University with a B.A. in Education.

Ms. Sohn is licensed to practice in Ontario, Canada.

◎ Education

- Faculty of Law, University of British Columbia, LL.B. (2005)
- Exchange Program, Faculty of Law, National University of Singapore (2005)
- Ontario Institute for Studies in Education, University of Toronto, M.A. (2002)
- Ewha Womans University, B.A. (1997)
- Exchange Program, Thiel College, Pennsylvania (1995-1996)

◎ Experience

- Yulchon LLC (2011-present)
- Associate, Holman Fenwick Willan, Singapore (2009-2011)
- Associate, Watson, Farley & Williams, Singapore (2008-2009)
- Associate, Hogan Lovells Lee & Lee, Singapore (2006-2008)
- Student-At-Law, Stikeman Elliott, Toronto, Canada (2005-2006)

◎ Representative Matters

- Represented Kumho Asiana Plaza Saigon Company Limited in its equity sale to Mapletree Investment in Singapore in reviewing the existing syndicated credit facility agreement and security documents with focus on refinancing transaction (2016)
- Acted for Chenavari Investment in connection with the sale of NPL to Taeheung (2016)
- Represented CK Partners relating to the Volcker Rule compliance in connection with the proposed investment structure (2016)
- Acted for BMWFSK regarding the issuance of KRW130billion unsecured bonds (2015)
- Acted for E-land Fashion China Holdings relating to its syndicated loan facility arranged by SCB with focus on the Korean parent's provision of share pledge and guarantee (2015)
- Acted for Hana Bank in reviewing and advising on the existing financing agreements in relation to the merger with KEB (2015)
- Acted for KDB in relation to the establishment of Volcker Rule compliance program (2015)
- Acted for BMWFSK regarding the issuance of KRW150billion unsecured bonds (2014)

- Acted for Oaktree Capital relating to provision of share pledge and guarantee in connection with the loans provided to Molycorp Korea's foreign affiliates (2014)
- Acted for Unison Capital relating to the acquisition of Gongcha Korea (2014)
- Acted for E-land Italy relating to its syndicated loan facility arranged by DB with focus on the Korean parent's provision of share pledge and guarantee (2014)
- Acted for KOFC in reviewing the existing credit facilities relating to certain business transfer to Kexim and merger with KDB (2014)
- Acted for E-land Asia Holdings relating to its syndicated loan facility arranged by DB with focus on the Korean parent's provision of share pledge and guarantee (2014)
- Acted for POSCO regarding its investment in Roy Hill Project (2014)
- Acted for Hyundai Steel Company in relation to its merger with the cold-rolled coil division of Hyundai Hysco (2014)
- Represented NPS in relation to the investment in the funds managed by Torchlight Debt Opportunity Fund (2014)
- Acted for Stokke Korea in providing share pledge and guarantee relating to the parent company, NXMH AS' syndicated loans (2014)
- Acted for Kexim relating to Italy-based corporation, Motia's restructuring agreements (2014)
- Acted for Hyundai Hysco regarding USD30million floating rate notes dues 2016 (2013)
- Acted for Dongwon Enterprise relating to its guarantee in connection with the USD230million loan provided to Starkist Co (2013)
- Acted for RBS relating to the guarantee provided by Kexim in connection with the loan provided to Kexim Bank (UK) (2013)
- Acted for Woori Bank in connection with the loan provided by the syndicate arranged by Sumitomo Mitsui Banking Corporation (2013)
- Acted for Global Marine Finance relating to the settlement agreements ship financing provided to Geden Holdings and its subsidiaries (2013)
- Acted for E-land Fashion China Holdings relating to its syndicated loan facility arranged by SCB with focus on the Korean parent's provision of share pledge and guarantee (2013)

- Acted for Chenavari Investments regarding the bonds with warrants subscription issued by Airpark Korea (2013)
- Acted for Lotte Shopping regarding KRW321,200million USD-settled zero coupon EBs (2013)
- Represented NordLB relating to the refinancing provided to POSCO Energy in connection with the power plants in Incheon (2012)
- Acted for Metlife relating to its build-transfer-lease financing of Paju-Yangju Army Facilities (2012)
- Acted for Zespri Korea relating to its provision of a guarantee in relation to the loans provided to Zespri Group Limited (2012)
- Acted for AM Plus relating to the issuance of corporate bonds (2012)

Source: Yulchon LLC Website (November 10, 2017)